The Prestige S

Gelligaer

Michael Yelton

Dedicated to Joseph Alexander Yelton.

CONTENTS

Acknowledgements

All black and white photographs in the book are from the camera or collection of Roy Marshall to whom we record our thanks. We are grateful to David and Mary Shaw for their meticulous proof-reading of the text.

Michael Yelton
June 2011

Cover pictures
Front Cover: Longwell Green-bodied AEC Reliance No. 16, new in 1957, in the distinctive post-war red, green and grey livery at Cilfynydd Common on the ex-CMS service from Pontypridd to Bedlinog. (*R Marshall*)
Title Page: Number 11, later 1, (KNY 453) in its original condition with an outswept skirt and much beading. It was the first of four Duple-bodied AEC Regals delivered in 1950. (*G Lumb*)
Inside Front Cover Upper: Ex-demonstrator, STB 957C, a Leyland Panther with Willowbrook body is shown on the route to Rhymney Bridge from Gelligaer. It was bought by Gelligaer in 1967. (*G Lumb*)
Inside Front Cover Lower: Longwell Green-bodied Leyland PD2 of 1959, in revised livery, is at Bargoed. Number 21 is on the route to Newport via Caerphilly. (*G Lumb*)
Inside Rear Cover Upper: Leyland PS1 with Duple body was No. 1 in the fleet at the time this photograph was taken at the depot. It was one of four similar vehicles delivered in 1951. (*G Lumb*)
Inside Rear Cover Lower: Number 18, an AEC Regent III with lowbridge Bruce bodywork of 1949 is shown outside the Gelligaer depot. (*G Lumb*)
Rear Cover: By 1954 many operators were taking delivery of underfloor-engined vehicles but Gelligaer took delivery of a pair of AEC Regal IIIs with bodywork by Longwell Green. Number 2, which is shown at Ystrad Mynach, remained in service until 1967. (*G Lumb*)

INTRODUCTION

The Gelligaer Urban District Council transport undertaking was small, somewhat idiosyncratic in many respects, and also little known outside its immediate area. In some ways it had an identity problem, as Gelligaer itself is only a village, although one with a considerable history, and the main settlement within the borders of the Urban District, which was established in 1908, was Bargoed (in Welsh Bargod), which remained throughout the centre of bus operations, although the administrative offices were further south, in Park Road, Hengoed. Even Roy Marshall, a lifelong bus enthusiast who in 1966 was to become general manager of the transport undertaking, was confused on his first visit to the area in 1949 and travelled to Gelligaer village before finding that Bargoed was a more interesting place for spotting.

Gelligaer had previously been part of the Gellygaer and Rhigos Rural District, established in 1894, which was itself an odd authority as it comprised two parcels which were much separated by other districts including the town of Merthyr Tydfil. Also, since Gelligaer was then growing rapidly, while Rhigos remained agricultural, it was sensible to split the two.

The new Urban District comprised the old civil parish of Gelligaer, namely Bargoed and the surrounding settlements, Hengoed, which lay immediately to the south of Bargoed, part of the important junction town of Ystrad Mynach, which was immediately south again, and the remaining section of which was in Caerphilly, and the outlying village of Bedlinog, which lay some distance to the west of Bargoed and had some considerable affinity with Merthyr. Gellygaer (the spelling of which was corrected to the more linguistically correct Gelligaer in late 1952 and the latter spelling of which will be used throughout this book) was in the County of Glamorgan, but lay on the border with Monmouthshire, which was formed by the Rhymney River. The next district to the north was Rhymney, which was actually in Monmouthshire, as were Bedwellty and Mynyddislwyn, which lay on the opposite bank from Bargoed. The settlement of Pengam, between Bargoed and Hengoed, was actually partly in each of the two counties.

The environment was typical of the South Wales valleys: steep roads, including the notorious Bargoed Hill which led up from the town to Aberbargoed in Bedwellty UD, terraces along the sides of the hills, and many mines. Bargoed itself is an archetypical Valleys town which prospered when the mines were active and was built up around them. It did not exist until the mid-Nineteenth Century, but between 1901 and 1922 the population grew from about 4,500 to 12,500 as Bargoed pit, owned by Powell Duffryn, produced vast quantities of coal: on 23rd April 1909 a ten hour shift saw a record of over 4,020 tons hewn out of the ground. A vast slag heap, at one time said to be the largest in the world, grew around the mine. However, the golden years of the South Wales coal industry were over by the early 1920s and thereafter there was a steady but pronounced depopulation of the area, as in many other localities around. The population of the Urban District was 28,800 in 1908, 40,100 in 1914, and 48200 in 1926. It then fell to 41,000 in 1931, a period which coincided with the introduction of the Council's transport services, and by 1951 had decreased to 36,100, after which it stabilised.

The closure of Bargoed pit in June 1977, shortly after the end of the period of independent transport operation by Gelligaer had ended, began a long and steep period of general decline for the town, which has only recently begun to reverse as commuting to Cardiff from the area becomes more established. However, during the time when the local buses were in operation, Bargoed was a considerable shopping centre, with a large department store known as the Emporium, complete with its own substantial clock tower.

The centre of the town, and indeed the centre of the operations of Gelligaer UDC, was the steeply graded Hanbury (formerly Trafalgar) Square, on the main street. It is, in fact, a triangle rather than a square and navigating the sharp turn at the furthest point from the main street and coping with the gradients amid the traffic called for a high degree of skill on the part of the drivers. It was so configured in order that when the rain poured down, as it often does in that region, it would run off the steeply graded sides of the triangle and down the flattish main road, rather than flooding the shops opposite. However, this meant that buses, especially when they became longer and lower, sometimes had real problems negotiating the exit from the terminal stands.

There was considerable traffic as well, to and from Ystrad Mynach, where there was a hospital, a railway station and educational establishments, all of which brought passengers in. When the system developed to its full extent, there were four separate routes between Bargoed and Ystrad Mynach, one of which went through the small but historically significant village of Gelligaer itself, which has a castle and a notable church. The other large pit in the district was Penallta, between Ystrad Mynach and Gelligaer, which was also on that route and was sunk in 1905. Bedlinog was somewhat isolated by its position, and it too had its own colliery, Taff Merthyr, which was not dug until after the First World War and was a model for many constructed thereafter. At Deri, above Bargoed, was the Groesfaen pit, which was taken over by Powell Duffryn in 1920, in which year they sank their last substantial mine in the area, Ogilvie, also near Deri.

There were a number of railways in the area, although as with so many other parts of South Wales they had been constructed with the primary purpose of transporting coal to the docks at Cardiff, Newport and Barry, and passenger traffic was of secondary importance. The Great Western line from Pontypool Road to Neath ran across the region from east to west and had stations at Hengoed and at Nelson & Llancaiach. At Hengoed it ran across and over the Rhymney Railway which connected Cardiff and Caerphilly with Bargoed and Rhymney, running right up the valley in direct competition with the buses when they were introduced. The line was then extended to Rhymney Bridge where it met the Heads of the Valleys line from Merthyr to Brynmawr. The line from Cardiff to Rhymney is still open and after a long period in which it was permitted to decay it has now been revitalised and carries an increasing commuter traffic. At Bargoed there was a branch to Darren & Deri which continued over horrendous gradients as the Brecon & Merthyr Railway line to Dowlais and Merthyr, with a station at Fochriw. Finally, the Great Western and Rhymney Railways built a joint line from Nelson & Llancaiach up to Dowlais Cae Harris, with a station at Bedlinog.

Because Bargoed lies in the Rhymney Valley, routes out of the town to the east and west were steep climbs, although Gelligaer never ran up and down Bargoed Hill itself. On the other side of the valley, the route up to Deri and then in its final form down from there to Pontlottyn, involved very considerable strains on the vehicles, accentuated in bad weather.

The commencement of operation by Gelligaer was a protracted business. As set out in detail in the following chapter, although the necessary Act of Parliament was obtained in 1920, there were thereafter frequent delays and turns in policy, mostly as a result of financial pressures and fears, and it was not until 1928 that services actually started.

The end was much less prolonged. Under the Local Government Act 1972, which took effect on 1st April 1974, the Urban District of Gelligaer ceased to exist. The original intention had been that the area be transferred into Monmouthshire, which became Gwent. However, in the event most of the district was transferred from the historic county of Glamorgan to the new county of Mid-Glamorgan, and incorporated into the new Rhymney Valley District Council, which also included most of the former Caerphilly Urban District from Glamorgan as well as Bedwas & Machen and Rhymney Urban Districts and part of Bedwellty, all of which had previously been in Monmouthshire. The Bedlinog area became part of Merthyr Tydfil. The headquarters of the new authority was in Hengoed, at the former Gelligaer UD offices. In due course yet a further reorganisation took place and the area became part of the new Caerphilly District. By that time, the only direct involvement of the Council with transport was in the former Islwyn Borough Transport, which originated with the West Monmouthshire Omnibus Board: Rhymney Valley's own operation collapsed after over-expanding after deregulation. The Islwyn operation has itself now been sold.

HISTORY OF THE UNDERTAKING 1928-45

Gelligaer was late in the day in commencing its transport operations. As with most of its neighbouring areas, there was no tram or trolleybus system: the volumes of traffic available were insufficient to justify substantial investment in infrastructure. Further, the area was poor and the Council was constantly short of money. Again, in company with its neighbours, the undertaking was run on a shoestring, although it seems to have been rather more prosperous than its constantly penurious neighbour, the West Mon Omnibus Board.

In the immediate post-First World War period, Gelligaer had toyed with the idea of starting its own services: at the same time, Caerphilly was beginning operations and Bedwas & Machen were well on the way to starting. It was not, however, until 1926 that the West Monmouthshire Omnibus Board was granted its own Act of Parliament and began its services.

Gelligaer had begun thinking about operating as early as 1st July 1919, and possibly even before then. At a meeting of the Council on that date, it was resolved that the Law and Parliamentary Committee be "again instructed to prepare and promote a Bill in Parliament authorising the Council to purchase and run throughout their area a service of motor buses". The use of the word "again" obviously indicates that there had been an earlier such request, but the details remain obscure. Nothing immediately occurred and on 2nd September 1919 the mover raised it again and it was directed that a meeting of the Committee take place as soon as possible. It in fact took place on 16th September 1919 and a recommendation was then made to the full Council to promote the necessary Bill. At that stage matters appeared to be progressing with speed and on 30th September 1919 it was agreed that a surveyor be employed temporarily to assist in the preparation of the Bill. Various councillors were anxious that powers for the widening and strengthening of some local bridges were included in it. Then it was suggested that an "expert tramway engineer" be engaged to advise, and this was to be Mr JB Hamilton, the experienced and well-respected general manager of Leeds City Transport. There followed, on 2nd December 1919, a special meeting of the Council at which, after considerable dissension, a motion that the Council apply for the now drafted Act to enable operations to commence was passed. The decision and its implementation was a matter of considerable local controversy and on 9th December 1919 there was yet a further meeting finally to approve the draft and on 6th January 1920 it was again necessary to obtain confirmation of the desirability of proceeding: this was after the Bill had been deposited. Thus was the way of small local authorities, in which personalities ruled much of what occurred and politics was often conducted on that basis, especially here where the Labour Party was throughout dominant and there was little effective organised opposition in the Council.

A final problem then reared its head. On 12th January 1920 there was a meeting of electors at which it appears that fewer than 30 people turned up. However, by a narrow majority a motion to delete the powers to run buses in the Bill was carried and it was then decided to put the matter to a local poll. However, there then appears one of the many inexplicable gaps which occur from time to time in all such bodies. It does not seem that the poll was ever taken although the concern was clearly over the financial implications and it appears that Mr Hamilton's report was not very optimistic on that score. On 4th August 1920 the Bill was passed in unamended form.

The Act of Parliament which gave the Council the power to run its transport undertaking, as with many such Acts which predated the Road Traffic Act 1930, was extremely restrictive in its terms. Once the 1930 Act was passed, all existing municipal operators were given powers to run anywhere within their own area and, with the consent of the local authority involved, into any other area. The 1920 Act on the other hand gave Gelligaer Urban District Council, by section 33(1), the right to run services only within its own area and also from Ystrad Mynach to Nelson, Trelewis and Bedlinog Square, but not so as to oppose Caerphilly UDC from so running: the road from Ystrad Mynach to Nelson was within their area. Gelligaer was also given the right, with the consent of the relevant local authority, to run into other areas in Glamorgan only. Under Section 39 of the Act it was permitted to enter into joint agreements with any company or undertaking for the purposes of its operations.

There then seems to have been some apathy after the frequent meetings over the Bill, and on 13th December 1920 a subcommittee meeting to consider buses was cancelled as there was no quorum. However, by January 1921 the Council's Surveyor had reported to the Public Works Committee, to the effect that AEC, Garford, Leyland, Palladium, Straker Squire, Thornycroft and Tilling Stevens were all interested in providing vehicles, the last being of the petrol-electric type.

The routes proposed in 1920 were Ystrad Mynach-Nelson-Bedlinog (much of the route of which was actually within Caerphilly's area) and Pengam-Bargoed-Deri. At that time the "New Road" from Pengam onward to Ystrad Mynach, which greatly improved local communications, had not been built. Construction of it commenced later in 1920 and cost a very substantial amount, including as it did the provision of a new bridge over the railway.

In December 1920 AEC sent a K type double-decker and a single-decker for trials: Palladium, a now-forgotten manufacturer, offered a discount and then sent a demonstrator with a special springing system and the Surveyor suggested looking also at a petrol-electric Tilling Stevens, as used already by Caerphilly, which had begun its running in early 1920.

By March 1921, however, the Surveyor was asked instead to ascertain the cost of one small bus, for the Bedlinog service, on the grounds that a great deal of money could be saved in relation to road repairs by using a 20-seater rather than a larger vehicle. He researched the cost of a Garford, which would have cost £1,200 and would have required a temporary garage. By then the proposal had been made even more modest and was only to connect Bedlinog with Nelson & Llancaiach Station, Trelewis, which was nearer to the outer terminus than Nelson village would have been, and strictly on an experimental basis. It was pointed out that running a service with only one vehicle was precarious, because of the possibility of a breakdown. A garage in Bargoed was then inspected and it was reported that it was suitable for single-deck buses, but it was resolved to defer consideration of its acquisition: that decision

seems to reflect that the Council had rapidly lost enthusiasm for running buses once the potential costs became clear.

However, it was consistently agreed that outside private operators should not be permitted to run into the Council's area, until in October 1921 it was suddenly resolved to permit ET Jones (later Jones Brothers, who traded as Commercial Motor Services), of Treharris, to operate from Bedlinog to Nelson. This decision marked a full scale retreat from the idea of the operation of services by the Council itself, and was confirmed by a resolution on 8th November 1921, that favourable consideration be given to various applications to run within the area, subject to approval of time and fare tables and the use of pneumatic tyres, the need for which became almost an obsession. In those pre-Judicial Review days, local authorities were able to hand down apparently arbitrary decisions without giving reasons, although on one occasion Gelligaer was threatened with a writ of mandamus (to compel them to act in accordance with their duty) to make them grant licences.

It is typical of the way in which small local authorities then operated that the major change of policy demonstrated by these decisions was never formally minuted. However, by late 1921 formal conditions were drafted for the running of such services by other operators. The councillors had developed very cold feet, even though one of them suggested that a sound reason for the local authority running its own services was that members themselves could more easily get to its meetings.

The Council thus proceeded to grant a variety of applications to different operators for services in and around the area, for which they themselves held powers which they were not then using. The licences were generally granted for 12 months only and some, particularly one granted to E Snow and Sons of Merthyr, were not renewed, although his was later reinstated. In November 1925 a separate Motor Charabanc Service Committee was set up and bye-laws were drafted by the clerk to the Council to regulate such applications.

However, in June 1925, while these matters were going forward and almost at the same time as there was a comprehensive consideration of outside operators' licences, a subcommittee was appointed to once again consider the question of operation by the Council. The subcommittee reported that four buses should be purchased and that a garage be erected on allotment land at Vere Street, Gilfach, just south of Bargoed. On 1st December 1925 the main committee decided to look for premises for use as a garage and to start this time with a Bargoed-Ystrad Mynach direct service: the New Road was by then completed. On 29th December 1925, only a few weeks after the bye-laws to permit others to run in the area had been considered, it was resolved to borrow £10,000 (a very considerable sum at that time for a local authority such as this) for the purposes of financing the Council's own operation, the viability of which had been seriously damaged by the decisions of the four years prior to that date. However, it was recorded that it appeared that the public would favour municipal operation.

The main architect of this U-turn in policy seems to have been Councillor Moses C Price, who appears to have been something of a livewire in his committee work, constantly proposing motions, many unfavourable to the private operators. He was a mainstay of the Council for a number of years, but did not stand in 1936 and died that year. Another stalwart was Ness Edwards (1897-1968), who was born in Abertillery, was a conscientious objector in the First World War because of his support for international socialism, and then became full time lodge secretary at Penallta pit. In 1939 he was elected as MP for Caerphilly (a constituency which included Gelligaer): he held the seat until his death many years later. His predecessor as MP, Morgan Jones, had also graduated to the House of Commons from membership of the Gelligaer UDC.

The real force on the Council before the war was, however, Thomas Evans (1897-1963), a former miner who then ran a dairy in Pengam. He was first elected in 1927 and became the leader of the dominant Labour group, resigning his seat only in 1950. In the meantime, he had been elected to Glamorgan County Council, of which he became chairman of the finance committee for many years, and he was also involved in many other public bodies.

There was a strong ideological, rather than strictly economic, motivation for local authority or publicly controlled transport, here as elsewhere in the South Wales area, tinged with an attachment to Protestant Nonconformity. It was symbolic that for the early years Russian Oil Products Ltd supplied the fuel for the buses. Many outsiders, on the other hand, expressed financial pessimism about the prospect of the Council operating its own undertaking, particularly the Ministry of Transport.

On 15th February 1926 the proposition that £10,000 be borrowed from the Municipal Finance Corporation to finance the undertaking was accepted. It was agreed to look at a garage at Ystrad Mynach (owned by the Blackwood (Monmouthshire) Motor Company, which had just sold its services to the Griffin Motor Company) and a potential site near the viaduct at Hengoed. Griffin was one of a large number of associated and interlinked companies involving the Watts family of Lydney, which eventually became Red & White.

Councillor Price wanted double-deckers to be purchased and asked specifically for estimates for them to be obtained. However, when the West Monmouthshire Omnibus Board was formed later that year, one of the provisions was that they take on the leased garage at Ystrad Mynach previously used by the Blackwood Motor Company, and so it at first it appeared to have passed away from Gelligaer. The Board, however, not requiring the garage, offered to lease it to their neighbours for £50 per annum, then to either sell or lease it, but after initial interest this was refused and West Mon soon, in fact, disposed of it.

Once again there was an unexplained delay in proceeding with the Council's own plans, but in July 1927 it was resolved to attempt to purchase the buses used by the substantial undertaking of Lewis & James of Newbridge and by two local operators, Mrs EK Matthews, who traded as Ystrad Saloon Coaches, and Mrs E Waters, who traded as Amber Bus Service as successor to WT Waters, both of Ystrad Mynach, on the route from Bargoed to Ystrad Mynach via the New Road: the two small businesses also ran via Gelligaer village. Nothing happened, however, not least because the Council had no garage available and there was yet another hiatus.

In June 1928 however, it was resolved to attempt to adapt the Council's existing stores building at Gilfach so that it could take four buses. At the same time, contact was made by Mrs Waters indicating a willingness to sell. In complete contradiction to its resolution of a year before, the Council said it was not interested in dealing with her.

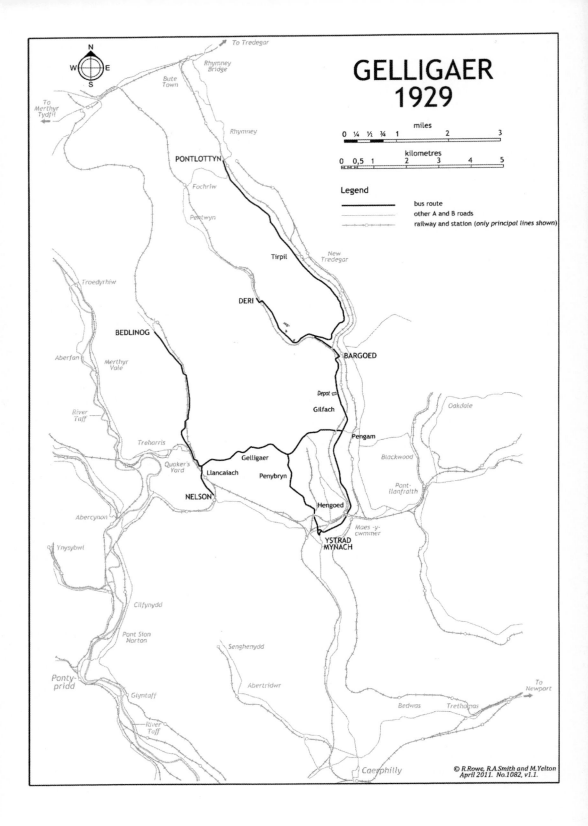

GELLIGAER
1929

miles

0 ¼ ½ ¾ 1   2   3

kilometres

0 0,5 1   2   3   4   5

Legend

— bus route
— other A and B roads
— railway and station (only principal lines shown)

N
W   E
S

To Tredegar

Rhymney Bridge

Bute Town

To Merthyr Tydfil

Rhymney

PONTLOTTYN

Fochriw

Pentwyn

Troedyrhiw

Tirpil

New Tredegar

DERI

BEDLINOG

Aberfan

Merthyr Vale

BARGOED

River Taff

Treharris

Depot

Gilfach

Oakdale

Quaker's Yard

Gelligaer

Pengam

Blackwood

Llancaiach

Penybryn

Pont-llanfraith

NELSON

Hengoed

Abercynon

Maes-y-cwmmer

YSTRAD MYNACH

Ynysybwl

Cilfynydd

Pont Sion Norton

Senghenydd

Pontypridd

Glyntaff

Abertridwr

To Newport

Bedwas

Trethomas

River Taff

Caerphilly

© R.Rowe, R.A.Smith and M.Yelton
April 2011. No.1082, v1.1.

8

On 10th July 1928 it was agreed to ask Leyland, Daimler and Vulcan (the latter through the agency of Hall Lewis of Cardiff, who were dealers as well as bodybuilders) to supply demonstrators: after all the vacillations of the previous nine years, matters were at last moving forward. After that demonstration, it was resolved to purchase four Leyland Tigers at £1,485 each and to commence services from Bargoed to Ystrad Mynach via New Road and via Gelligaer. The first manager appointed was H McNaul, who was to take on that role in addition to his existing responsibilities as electrical engineer. It was also agreed that two vehicles be housed in Bargoed fire station (the fire service was at that time run by the local authority) and two in a garage below Bargoed Market at a rent of 15s per week, but shortly afterwards it was decided to build a garage at Aeron Place, Gilfach. In the meantime, the suggestion that the market area be used was rescinded and instead a garage in Maesygraig Street, Gilfach, was rented temporarily, later substituted by a garage in Bargoed.

By this time there were eight operators running within the Council's area. These included the West Mon Board, which had acquired various routes within its area, including one from Lewis & James, part of which linked Markham with Aberbargoed, on the Monmouthshire side of the Rhymney Valley, way above Bargoed itself. Lewis & James had wanted to start a through service from Markham down into Bargoed, but in June 1926 Gelligaer had refused consent. When the Board took over, the consent was given (after two initial refusals) and the famous, or notorious, Bargoed Hill route began operation at 3pm on 31st May 1927, originally in the afternoons only. When Gelligaer did eventually start running, it never sought to acquire any share of the hill route, no doubt because of the very considerable difficulties it would have posed: thus the best known route into the area was never operated by the local authority itself.

Also running in Gelligaer at that time, apart from Matthews and Waters, were Lewis & James, who ran a through service Newbridge-Pontllanfraith-Blackwood-Bargoed-Deri and in addition on the short Ystrad Mynach-Bargoed service. In 1925 Lewis & James had sold out to the National Electric Construction Company and in due course their operations formed one of the

constituent parts of Western Welsh, set up by the BET and the Great Western Railway, which was to become one of the two largest company operators in the area. The other was Red & White, which at this time was not yet in existence, but two of its predecessors were Valleys Transport, which ran from Bargoed north along the valley through Pontlottyn and Rhymney to terminate at Rhymney Bridge, where the valley met the main road from Merthyr to Tredegar and an interchange point existed, and Aberdare Motor Services, who ran from Aberdare to Bargoed via Nelson and Gelligaer. A third operator which also eventually (in 1935) became part of Red & White was Imperial Motor Services of Abercynon, who ran from Pontypridd to Bedlinog via two routes and had absorbed, earlier in 1928, the operations of Snow of Merthyr. Finally, Jones Brothers, later trading as Commercial Motor Services Ltd, of Treharris, also ran between Pontypridd and Bedlinog.

On 9th September 1928 (the exact date is not entirely clear from the Council's minutes, despite the proliferation of other trivia, but is given in the official history of the area and elsewhere) operations were finally commenced, in unusual circumstances: the first five vehicles were not owned by the UDC, but were Leylands previously owned by Eastern Valleys of Pontnewynydd, which had passed via South Wales Commercial Motors, dealers in Cardiff, to Hall, Lewis and Company. It was at first expected that Leyland themselves would supply temporary vehicles pending the arrival of the order, but thereafter it was agreed that Hall Lewis provide them at £1 per day per bus. Urgency seems to have taken over from delay.

In November 1928 the four new Leyland TS2 models with Leyland dual-door bodywork arrived (TX 6324, 6326, 6367 and 6369) and in December of that year they were joined by two small Albions with Hall, Lewis front-entrance bodies (TX 6459/60): Albion, Dennis and Thornycroft had been asked for estimates. The cost of the new vehicles was £855 10s each. The four Leylands were delivered in a livery of red and cream, which did not distinguish the Council's buses markedly from many others in the area. However, the two Albions introduced a new colour scheme of red, white and green, the constituents of the Welsh national flag. It was applied so that the lower part of the vehicle was red, the waistline was green, with the name of the undertaking on it, and the upper part was white. As well as being attractive, this was unusual and marked out the vehicles immediately.

The first routes were indeed from Bargoed to Ystrad Mynach via the two alternative routes, in competition with Lewis & James and with the two local operators.

Another early service, begun in October 1928, was from Bargoed to Deri, on which there was initially strong competition from Lewis & James, with their through route from Newbridge. Meanwhile, however, the West Mon Board wanted to reach Bargoed on its own service from Blackwood, which at that time terminated at Pengam, thus not achieving the main centre of potential traffic. Pressure was put on Lewis & James by West Mon under the terms of the agreements scheduled to the Act setting up the Board, and this led to a reorganisation in 1929, in which it acquired the Blackwood-Bargoed section of the Newbridge-Deri route from Lewis and James. The Bargoed-Deri section, which was difficult to operate and was of no interest to the local authorities on the Monmouthshire side of the river, was released to Gelligaer, thus ending the competition on it. West Mon was thus able to run into Bargoed on a second route, following the hill service.

In November 1928 the Council started a service from Bargoed north along the main road to Pontlottyn, on which there was, of course, competition from Valleys Motor Services. That competition was to be long lasting, although for many years the Council and Red & White, as successors to Valleys, appeared to pretend that the other did not exist so far as their timetables were concerned, albeit behind the scenes there were frequent interchanges in relation to co-ordination of timetables, interavailability of tickets, and the like.

A further service begun in the early months was Bargoed-Gelligaer-Nelson-Bedlinog, commencing December 1928, on which there was competition from Aberdare Motor Services on the Bargoed-Nelson section and from Imperial Motor Services and Jones Brothers on the Nelson-Bedlinog leg. Initially, in August 1928 Gelligaer had resolved that there be two routes, Bedlinog to Ystrad Mynach via Gelligaer and Bedlinog to Hengoed via Nelson, and although that proposal was not implemented it appears that until April 1929 separate services Nelson-Bedlinog and Bargoed-Gelligaer-Bedlinog were run, which were then combined, so that a double run to Nelson was incorporated. Certainly in later years all services between Bargoed and Gelligaer also had a short double run down Oxford Street, Glyngaer (an area also known locally as White City), to a turning circle, but it is not clear when that began.

It was a time when across the whole country there was a great expansion of bus routes and much new housing. In Gelligaer there were new housing schemes at Heolddu, near Bargoed, and at Graig Hengoed, but no new services were provided to them at this time. However, as soon as the Council began running itself, it simultaneously began to take a much harder line against any of the other operators who ran vehicles or used drivers who were not licensed.

Very shortly after operations began, Mr McNaul indicated that he wished to relinquish his role with the transport department and it was decided to employ a full time manager, although he continued in charge until the appointment could be made. At this time the transport garage was built in Aeron Place by the Council's own workmen.

In early January 1929 the expansion plans continued with a decision to buy two Thornycrofts for a total of £2,595 and with temporary vehicles being supplied pending their delivery. However, in early February 1929 firstly Mrs Waters then Mrs Matthews indicated that they were prepared to sell out, the former for £1,750 and the latter for £1,500. Much of the sum due to Amber Motor Services was actually paid direct to Hall Lewis, to whom Mrs Waters was heavily indebted.

On 22nd March 1929 it was agreed, after the cessation of the two small operators, to run through services Deri-Bargoed-Ystrad Mynach and Pontlottyn-Bargoed-Gelligaer-Ystrad Mynach. In the same month Mr F Fabian of Pyle, near Bridgend, was appointed as the first manager.

One of the consequences of the takeover was that there was an influx of vehicles. Ystrad Saloon Coaches provided three AECs with United dual-entrance bodies, and Amber Services a Lancia and a Thornycroft, both bodied by Hall Lewis. The existing order for two Thornycrofts was consequently cancelled, but in lieu one was ordered for £1,250 and it was suggested that AEC

There are very few pre-war pictures of the fleet. However, one of the first batch of vehicles, No. 3 (TX 6367), a Leyland TS2 with Leyland dual-entrance bodywork, is captured here.

The offside of the first batch of vehicles is captured in this view of No. 4 (TX 6369) on the Bargoed-Pontlottyn service.

NY 7501, acquired from Matthews, be taken in part exchange, although in fact it was then re-engined but shortly thereafter disposed of. The difficult economic conditions, and in particular the grave problems in mining, were reflected in a decision in June 1929 to use one-man operation if required (particularly on the Bedlinog route) and to pay a premium of 1d per hour to drivers of one-man vehicles.

The year 1930 was a critical one in the history of the undertaking. It was, of course, the year when the Road Traffic Act was passed, although it did not come into effect until 1st April 1931: it was thus necessary to plan for the new regime, and to that end agreement was reached with Valleys and Aberdare (which were incorporated that year into the new Red & White company) to coordinate fares and timetables. In the pre-war period Red & White ran Bargoed-Pontlottyn-Rhymney Bridge on the ex-Valleys service and Bargoed-Gelligaer-Nelson-Aberdare or Pontypridd on the ex-Aberdare service as well as Pontypridd-Nelson-Bedlinog on the former Imperial route.

In addition, there was an undercurrent of discontent in the Council in relation to the running of the transport department, probably because Mr Fabian had no previous experience of that type of work. In June 1930 he resigned, perhaps because of pressure put on him to do so, and the post was advertised, with a specific requirement that experience in a municipal undertaking was required. In addition a detailed schedule of the duties of the transport manager was drawn up.

The first competition failed to produce a satisfactory applicant, and the position was readvertised. Mr Fabian agreed to remain in post until a successor was found and in July 1930 Edward Bernard Blainey was appointed. Although he had no experience of municipal undertakings, he was then 48, and, after service in the First World War, he had run a bus service in his home town, Barry between 1922 and 1925, where there were a multitude of independent operators. He then became a member, then the secretary, of Barry Associated Motors Ltd, a consortium of some of the independents, which went into liquidation in 1930.

Edward Blainey brought a new professionalism to the running of the Gelligaer transport department although, as with other small undertakings, he suffered from over-management by the Transport Committee, which insisted on taking the final decision as to who should be employed, even down to office boys and typists. Eventually, a system developed in which there were two separate committees of the Council, one to deal with general transport matters and the other, the Motor Omnibus Appeals Board, to hear appeals from disciplinary decisions of the manager, who was something of a stickler in that regard. In May 1931 he dismissed six men from the garage staff for "general neglect of duty". In July 1931 the first inspector was appointed.

As early as September 1930 the new manager was advocating the purchase of new vehicles, and over the next few years he pursued the expansion and modernisation of the fleet, with a particular emphasis on the provision of diesel instead of petrol engines. The first new purchases, however, five AEC Regals which arrived in 1931, the first three with bodies by Metcalfe and the remaining two by Weymann, were the last new petrol-engined vehicles in the fleet, although fairly shortly all save one which had a very short life were re-engined to run on diesel. All had dual entrances.

In January 1931 it was resolved to attempt to extend the existing Pontlottyn service to Rhymney and after a site visit on 3rd March 1931 it was agreed to apply to go right through to Rhymney Bridge, which had little traffic potential itself save as an interchange point but ensured that the whole of the township of Rhymney was served. Further, although the town of Rhymney was in Monmouthshire, a northern projection of Gelligaer Urban District just took in the Rhymney Bridge terminus and also encompassed a considerable distance of the main road on towards Dowlais. Consideration was even given to running through to Dowlais and Merthyr along that road, but in May 1931 it was decided to defer that suggestion, together with a projected extension beyond Deri to Fochriw and a proposed new route between Bargoed and Ystrad Mynach via Cefn Hengoed.

Mr Blainey did not want the West Mon Board to increase its service between Blackwood and Bargoed, which had become busier after its extension from Pengam, and Gelligaer began operating on the route. He wanted an equal share of the service.

On 14th October 1931 the Traffic Commissioners, sitting in Newport, heard the various applications. That to run to Rhymney

Bridge was granted, and operations began on 21st December 1931 after a coordinated timetable had been agreed with Red & White. The through route from Rhymney Bridge to Ystrad Mynach took just under an hour and was always the best patronised of the undertaking's services: it normally ran about every thirty minutes, and although it served a number of settlements there were quite long stretches without much population. On the Blackwood route, the Traffic Commissioners ordered that the Board run the morning service and the two operators jointly run the afternoon service, so that the Board had a 3:1 proportion of journeys run over the day. Since both these new routes involved running into Monmouthshire, Gelligaer had no capacity to operate them under their own Act of 1920, but were given that power by the general provisions of the Road Traffic Act 1930.

Gelligaer, in company with other South Wales municipalities, applied to run excursions and tours from their area, but that application was refused, as were those of all the others.

The other significant change in local traffic arrangements at this time was that Western Welsh were given permission to link up their existing Ystrad Mynach-Bargoed service, which they had inherited from Lewis & James, to their new Newport-Bedwas-Caerphilly service and from 1932 they ran though Newport-Bedwas-Caerphilly-Ystrad Mynach-Bargoed, which not only provided many new connections but in the long term was to be a very important factor in the development of traffic patterns for the municipalities of Bedwas & Machen and of Gelligaer.

Mr Blainey then turned his attention to access to Cardiff. It was decided to apply to extend some journeys on the Rhymney Bridge service as expresses to Cardiff via Caerphilly, but after a meeting with Cardiff and Caerphilly Councils and West Mon, who were the joint operators on the long Cardiff-Caerphilly-Ystrad Mynach-Blackwood-Markham service introduced in 1930, it was agreed that in lieu of a through service connections would be offered at Ystrad Mynach for transfers between the two routes, and that a common front would be erected against any attempt by Western Welsh to run from Bargoed to Cardiff. The connections required a short extension by Gelligaer in Ystrad Mynach, from the Beech Hotel down Commercial Street to the Royal Oak, and this was granted in early 1933, so that alternate journeys from Rhymney Bridge met the joint service there. Through bookings were accepted and sums were remitted to Cardiff Corporation, which operated a clearing system on behalf of itself and the other two operators.

Simultaneously, there were developments on the vehicle front. The garage in Gilfach was already proving inadequate, and it was resolved in November 1931 to extend it. At about the same time an AEC Regent double-decker, probably JF 223, was taken on demonstration, but none was ordered: there were, in any event, potential difficulties as the garage would not take such vehicles.

Although times were still bad economically, the undertaking was doing reasonably well. The year ending March 1932 saw a small profit of £800, the first time this had happened, and thereafter profits were accrued for many years successively. The outlook was so much better that in early 1932 it was agreed to buy a new single-decker out of revenue rather than by financing it with a loan. The new vehicle cost £1,599 10s and had a diesel (or as it was then termed "crude oil") engine, the first with a South Wales municipality. It was a six-wheeled AEC Renown with Weymann dual-entrance body which seated 38, a considerable increase on what was otherwise available and an alternative to a double-decker. In December 1932 AEC agreed to lend a vehicle for the busy Christmas period.

In that year it was also agreed that some journeys should be introduced between Bargoed and Ystrad Mynach via Cefn Hengoed, on Fridays and Saturdays only.

The progress of the undertaking was interrupted by an unofficial strike in January 1933. This was relatively unusual, because jobs on the buses were sought after and not readily given up, they were regarded as being much easier than work in the pit. However, the Transport Committee, although ideologically and politically far to the left, was very unsympathetic to the men and even threatened legal proceedings. In 1935 the Council itself was the subject of such proceedings, the nature of which is not entirely clear but seems to have involved the right to refuse entry to its vehicles, which began with an injunction application before a Judge in London and ended with a hearing at the Glamorgan Assizes, which Gelligaer lost.

Meanwhile, Mr Blainey was able to continue with his modernisation plans. In May 1933 it was decided to convert one of the Leylands to diesel and in July it was agreed to buy three new vehicles from AEC for a total of £4,417 10s. The first two were conventional AEC Regal 4 types with Weymann 32-seat rear-entrance bodies, but the manager was anxious that one of the orders should be for a revolutionary Q type, with side engine and increased seating capacity. The design was well ahead of its time and was not in the end a financial success for the manufacturers, but it was an unusual vehicle for a small municipality to purchase, particularly one which after the war was to develop a reputation for extreme conservatism in its vehicle specifications. On 21st November 1933 the manager reported to the Committee in favour of buying a Q type, but it alone would cost £1,847 so the earlier sanction was bound to be exceeded. The new bus, TG 8266, with a 39-seat centre-entrance body built by Short Brothers of Rochester, arrived in August 1934. The body was a modification by Shorts of their usual single-deck design as applied to half-cabs, and was somewhat angular. However, it was undoubtedly an impressive vehicle.

Perhaps to cut down on expenditure, another AEC Regal, MV 295, was hired in late 1933. It was probably the same vehicle as had been used the year before, but unlike then it was kept for some considerable time, and eventually, in May 1935, was sent to Sylvesters of Barry to be repainted in Gelligaer livery and was later purchased for stock.

In February 1934 it was agreed to seal up the front doors on dual-entrance vehicles, increasing the seating capacity. In May 1935 it was decided to convert the three remaining Leylands to diesel.

Development of new services at this time was not extensive. In late 1933 William L Williams of Rhymney Bridge applied unsuccessfully for permission to run a Bargoed-Deri-Fochriw-Pontlottyn service, and in September 1934 Gelligaer resolved to apply to extend two trips on Fridays and Saturdays beyond Deri to Fochriw, but this was not then followed through. However, it was then agreed that a new town service in Bargoed should be run to Heolddu Drive, with effect from 25th February 1935. The proposal to extend from Deri to Fochriw was resurrected and the application was heard on 17th April 1936, but

refused because of the opposition of the Great Western Railway, which had a station there on its line from Bargoed to Dowlais.

By late 1936 the Committee asked the manager to report on whether the next purchase should be a Leyland Tiger or a second AEC Q. A confusing series of events resulted, which is not unprecedented in local authority deliberations. On 6th October 1936 it was resolved to purchase a Leyland Tiger with oil engine, but on 3rd November 1936 this decision was rescinded. On 10th November 1936, after what was described as "a lengthy discussion" it was decided to buy a further Q type for £1,800, against which one of the elderly Leylands would be part exchanged. The Q arrived in January 1937 as BTX 113, with a Strachans centre-entrance body again seating 39. This was, in fact, the last non-London Q type constructed, and the only one with a Strachans body. The look of the vehicle as originally delivered was very different from the first Q, with an almost coach-like use of lining out and the green waist rail being extended down at the rear. It was a far better looking vehicle than its predecessor. Although sales of the Q type were very limited outside London, a number were sold to other operators in South Wales, including Red & White, Imperial Motor Services and Gough of Mountain Ash.

In September 1937 it was agreed that a further two vehicles were required, and in March 1938, after yet more extensive debate, the Committee voted by 11 to 8 to purchase the new buses from Leyland rather than AEC, at a cost of £1,492 10s each. It is noteworthy that heaters were specified and that cushions for the seats were also ordered: Gelligaer was unlike Aberdare UDC, which for many years used vehicles with wooden slatted seats because of contamination from coal on miners' clothes. It was also agreed that one should be purchased from revenue, and one by means of a loan. These appeared as DNY 448/9, Leyland TS8s with Strachans forward-entrance bodies, in June 1938.

The final pre-war purchases arrived in 1939, and were again the subject of considerable wrangling. In late 1938 it was agreed to buy two AECs, one coming from revenue as with the previous order. On 8th December 1938 it was decided to purchase only one AEC Regal, which was to cost £1,464 against which £25 would be treated as a contra for one of the 1928 Leyland Tigers. It was also

One of a pair of AEC Regals delivered in 1931 was No. 12 (TG 2590) which was delicensed and then rebuilt between 1947 and 1949. This picture was taken in 1950 and shows it at Bargoed.

This rather dark picture of No. 12, taken in 1951, is included because it shows the unsatisfactory garage in Aeron Place in its later years.

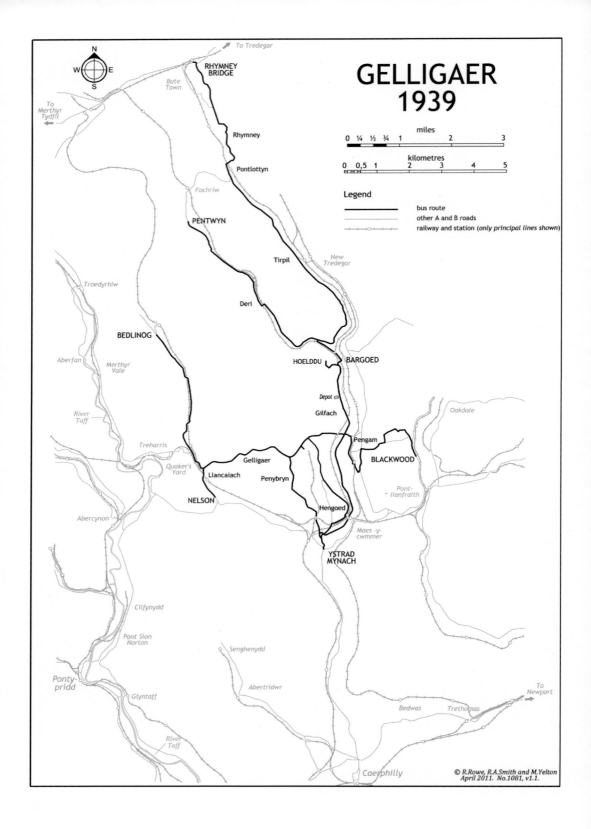

GELLIGAER
1939

agreed to ask Court Street Works Ltd, of Merthyr, to repair the bodies of two vehicles, possibly from the 1931 influx of Regals. The new Regal, DTX 652, appeared in March 1939 and also had a body by Strachans, but this time with a rear entrance.

In early 1939, with war looking possible, the issue of producer gas vehicles was raised. However, after a meeting with Sentinel of Shrewsbury, the proposed manufacturer, on 7th February 1939 it was decided that they were not a practicable proposition, no doubt because of the gradients. The issue of a second conventional vehicle was then raised again, and by 13-6 the Committee voted for a Leyland rather than a second AEC. This was ETG 77, another TS8 with a rear-entrance Strachans body, which came in August 1939.

The garage from which operations were run was extremely unsatisfactory. On 15th March 1938 it was agreed to purchase land adjacent to Lewis Grammar School, Pengam, in order to build a new garage there. A draft contract was in existence shortly thereafter, but the matter did not proceed and the cramped Aeron Place premises continued to be used.

In November 1937 a proposal to increase the Deri service to half hourly instead of hourly was deferred, but there were still complaints from those who lived beyond the terminus. In 1938 it was decided to apply to extend some journeys to Penybank and Pentwyn, the settlements immediately beyond Deri, but short of Fochriw, and permission was granted on 11th November 1938, for three years in the first instance.

As war broke out, Gelligaer still had grossly inadequate garage premises but it had a reasonably modern fleet, all of either AEC or Leyland manufacture. The onset of hostilities was not met with any enthusiasm locally: the deeply ingrained left wing cast of the Council is well demonstrated by the passing of a resolution that there should be no conscription of men without prior conscription of wealth.

As with most industrial areas, the war years saw the fleet hard worked and loadings very high. Services finished early. Mines and factories worked around the clock and there was no means of travel to many of them but bus. The Traffic Commissioners were superseded during hostilities and it became easier to achieve variations at relatively short notice.

In February 1940 it was agreed to increase services to Heolddu and to Deri by 50%: the latter route passed the substantial Groesfaen Colliery. On 6th July 1941 Sunday services on all routes were cut by 50% on orders from London but on 19th July 1942 Fochriw was finally reached by a two hourly service and the workings to Pentwyn ceased: this would require reconsideration once the wartime system of permits ended. The final wartime development was the improvement in the Cefn Hengoed service, which began in 1944, after which it generally ran every two hours. In December 1944 later evening services were again authorised.

There was, of course, no question during the hostilities of building a new garage. The roof was patched up early on, and in March 1942 the then revolutionary decision to employ female conducting staff was taken. It was decided that they must be at least 31 years old, although it is not clear why that age limit was imposed. The employment of conductresses also necessitated the rehousing of the tenant of the house next door, so that they could use it as a mess room.

Initially, the fleet was sufficient but by late 1940 it was resolved that new buses should be purchased from whatever source was available. In July 1942 it was definitely resolved to accept three new single-deckers and not to accept a double-decker on loan from London, as had apparently been offered and as was taken up by West Mon. A small Bedford was borrowed from Western Welsh for a time.

In early 1943 three Bedford OWBs with Duple bodywork to Utility standards arrived, FNY171-3, followed by a further similar vehicle in September, FNY 457, and three more, FNY 559, 612 and 875, the following year. However, 1944 also saw a real break from tradition with the arrival of the first two double-deckers ever owned by the undertaking, FNY 703/4, which had Daimler CWA6 chasses and Brush lowbridge bodies. The garage needed alteration to accommodate them so that there was a separate entrance leading only to an inspection pit at one end of the premises, but largely the double-deckers were simply parked in the street. In late 1944 the need for structural alterations was agreed, but that was subject to permit.

During the war, new vehicles were delivered in all-over grey or chocolate colour, and on others the existing livery was modified so that grey replaced white over the top half.

There were no other new vehicles delivered during the war, and in September 1944 one of the 1938 Leylands, DNY 448, was involved in a serious accident and its Strachans body had to be dismantled. It was not rebodied until 1950, although DNY 449 received a new body as early as 1946, the work in both cases being carried out by Burlingham. The first of the Q types had been withdrawn in 1942 but the second, BTX 113, was initially to have been rebodied externally. However, from late 1944 to early 1946 it was completely rebuilt by the Council itself to give it the appearance of a utility. It was noted that any new garage should incorporate a repair shop.

Wider matters also surfaced from time to time. The issue of whether or not a joint board should be set up to encompass the operations of Gelligaer, Caerphilly, Bedwas & Machen and West Monmouthshire was one which came up regularly through the years. In 1942 it made one of its periodic reappearances. Gelligaer councillors voted strongly in favour of the idea but neither then nor later did it proceed, not least because the members of the West Mon Board would have nothing to do with it. Local pride meant that the coming together of the undertakings had to wait until the reorganisation of local government under the Act of 1972.

The councillors also at about the same time, with scant regard for the obvious conflict of interest, voted reduced rate season tickets for themselves, to enable them to carry out their local authority duties.

The end of the war, here as in other places, saw an exhausted and rundown fleet having to cope with a hugely increased demand for travel as the population was released from the constrictions imposed by the conflict. However, traditional hostilities remained and in February 1945 there were complaints that Western Welsh were abstracting traffic on the New Road route: they were asked to consider moving their Bargoed terminus, but refused.

The AEC Q with Strachan body, No. 1, was substantially rebuilt by the Council between 1944 and 1946 and is shown here in Bargoed in 1949 bound for Deri, shortly after suffering an accident and not long before withdrawal.

Strachan-bodied Leyland TS8 of 1939 No. 4 was rebuilt by Bruce Coachworks in 1950 with a B34F body and is seen here at the Tiryberth garage in reconstructed condition.

The second Daimler was No. 7 (FNY 704) seen here in 1952 at Gilfach, also on the Rhymney Bridge service, with a Leyland Tiger in hot pursuit.

AEC Regal/Harrington No. 5 (FTG 846) is seen here after repainting from wartime drab, at Tiryberth depot.

One of the Leyland/Willowbrooks of 1947 is seen at Hanbury Square on the Bargoed local to the Heolddu Estate.

HISTORY OF THE UNDERTAKING 1945-74

At the end of hostilities, Gelligaer was running the following services, which did not then carry numbers:

Rhymney Bridge-Pontlottyn-Bargoed-Ystrad Mynach

Bargoed-Deri-Fochriw

Bargoed-Gelligaer-Ystrad Mynach

Bargoed-Cefn Hengoed-Ystrad Mynach

Bargoed-Heolddu

Bargoed-Gelligaer-Nelson-Bedlinog

Bargoed-Blackwood (jointly with West Mon)

The fleet then consisted of the two Daimler double-deckers with utility bodywork, the two Weymann-bodied AEC Regals of 1931, which had been rebuilt as rear-entrance only, the AEC Renown of 1932, which had been similarly rebuilt, the 1933 Regal, also so rebuilt, the two 1934 Regals, which were at the end of their useful life and were about to be withdrawn, the 1931 Regal which had originally been on long term loan and

was in a similar position, the second Q, which was in the process of having its body rebuilt, the two Leyland TS8s of 1938, one of which had just been rebodied and the other of which was out of action awaiting a new body, the AEC Regal and Leyland Tiger of 1939, and seven Bedford OWBs delivered during the war, a total of 21 vehicles, not all of which were then operational.

The years immediately following the war and through to about 1955 were a boom time for public transport here as elsewhere. The pent-up demand for travel which had not been satisfied during the war years was released and private motoring was still rare. Bus usage continued high in the South Wales Valleys after it began declining elsewhere, as wages were low and cars less often found than in other areas and there was a particular emphasis on late evening travel: the Gelligaer Transport Committee was constantly reporting overcrowding on the last buses, even during the week. The three other small municipal operators in the vicinity, Caerphilly, Bedwas & Machen and West Monmouthshire, all increased their fleets and also introduced comparatively large numbers of double-deckers. While Gelligaer also increased

A nearside view of the other 1949 Regent, No. 18 (HTX 397) at Tiryberth garage. West Mon took delivery of two similar vehicles in the same year.

its fleet, the number of double-deckers remained very small and the majority of the vehicles were half-cab single-deckers.

In September 1945 Mr Blainey died suddenly and WH Collins, his chief clerk, was appointed to act as manager for the time being: in December 1945 he was appointed permanently. One of his earliest tasks was to ensure that the wartime service provisions which had been agreed under the special procedure were confirmed by the Traffic Commissioner, and this he dealt with successfully.

The lot of the Transport Manager was not a very happy one as, here as elsewhere in the small South Wales municipal operators, the Transport Committee continued to insist on dealing with all appointments, even of garage cleaners and junior office staff, and on hearing details of disciplinary matters which had already been dealt with. The rather peculiar procedure evolved whereby the Committee, which nearly always seems to have upheld the Manager, retrospectively approved suspensions, dismissals and the like which he had imposed: the pre-war system of having a separate committee to deal with appeals from the Manager was discontinued. This insistence on interference on issues which should have been delegated meant that on occasion the wider picture was lost.

The first significant event in route development immediately after the war was the joint takeover in 1945 by Gelligaer, Caerphilly and Pontypridd UDCs and the West Monmouthshire Omnibus Board of the stage carriage operations of Jones Brothers (Treharris) Ltd, trading as Commercial Motor Service (CMS), which was by then a well established business with two basic routes, Pontypridd-Nelson-Bedlinog (Square) and Pontypridd-Treharris-Nelson-Ystrad Mynach-Blackwood. The former antedated the Road Traffic Act: the latter had been started in 1932 against the bitter opposition of West Mon, which always sought to keep outsiders out of Blackwood. The Jones undertaking had originally been offered for sale for £35,000 to Gelligaer alone, in March 1945, and they refused to proceed at that price, but decided to involve the three other eventual purchasers. Merthyr Borough Council, in the area of which the Jones garage lay, were not interested at all and the others brought in by Gelligaer were not interested at the original price: they speedily knocked it down to £25,000 and

acquired the business in November 1945 although the agreement between the four of them was not concluded until 4th February 1946. Gelligaer originally voted to go only to £20,000 but then agreed to go along with the others.

Although the purchase represented a rare common approach by the small local municipalities, the old territorial tensions remained. In late 1945 West Mon brought up the subject of its route to Abertysswg, which had been blocked by a landslip which has never, in fact, been cleared. In order to continue to run to that settlement, which was outside the area of either of the Urban Districts which set up the Board, it was necessary to run into Gelligaer's area: the latter strongly objected to this and for several years later, after the diversion was granted, complained about the wrongful picking-up of passengers.

The purchase of the CMS services was not in the long term a sensible proposition financially, particularly for Caerphilly as the routes were so distant from its garage. Gelligaer at least had an interest in serving Bedlinog as it was within its local government area. The four operators set up the Ex-CMS Joint Services Committee, which thereafter met quarterly.

Thereafter, the Pontypridd-Nelson-Bedlinog services were shared between Red & White (as successors to Imperial) on the one hand and the joint operators on the other. However, although each side ran every two hours, the intervals on the combined service initially alternated between thirty and ninety minutes. The service was extended beyond the Square to Hylton Terrace.

It does not appear that Gelligaer ran on the Blackwood service regularly and it was generally run by Caerphilly from one end and West Mon from the other, with Pontypridd running Sunday services. The Bedlinog service was principally run by Gelligaer, with Pontypridd running some weekend services. Pontypridd also ran some afternoon journeys between their home town and Treharris and Red & White also ran an additional and more regular hourly service between Pontypridd and Treharris.

The buses used by CMS on the stage services were divided between the purchasers. Gelligaer's allotment was a 1932 Dennis Lancet with Weymann body, formerly owned by Western Welsh, which they did not ever run in service, a 1934 Leyland TS6 with diesel engine which had been rebodied by Burlingham in January 1945, and a Bedford OWB dating from 1943. The latter two were welcome additions and the Tiger lasted another 11 years.

Another consequence of the end of the war and the return of men from the services was that in May 1946 it was said that 4 of the 5 conductresses taken on had been discharged: the last one remaining in service was a widow, and her case was considered by the full council, which resolved to dispense with her services also. Thereafter, the road staff was solidly male for very many years, an interesting reflection on attitudes in the region to employment. There was an employees' social club, but this was wound up in 1966.

Almost immediately following the return of peace, work began to replace the slatted seats of the utility vehicles with upholstered versions: although there were frequent complaints about miners and others workers soiling vehicles, the Council, unlike neighbouring Aberdare, did not order wooden seating after the war. The Council also had to contend with the adverse weather conditions which affected most of the country in 1947: on 5th March of that year all services had to be suspended. The worst-affected section of road was the then recently introduced extension from Fochriw to Pontlottyn, which was frequently impassable.

The immediate post-war years saw a considerable influx of vehicles into the fleet, which remained dominated by Leyland and AEC. In 1946 three new AEC Regals arrived, the first two of which (FTG 846 and 977) had Harrington forward-entrance bodies of a utility style with few refinements and came in the early summer. In November of that year a further Regal arrived, FTX 175, which had a Duple dual-purpose body which initially featured high-back coach type seats, which were later replaced by standard bus seats: its order seems to have been a last minute decision and the records do not disclose why this seating was fitted. The following year the supplier was changed to Leyland, because they could deliver more quickly, and in June three PS1/1 types arrived with Willowbrook bus bodies: that company was again chosen simply because of its ability to fulfil an order in difficult times. The livery adopted by this time was that of red, green and grey as used on some vehicles during the war, and this replaced the red, green and white used

before 1939. In July 1952, it was decided that the coat of arms should be applied to the waist rail. It depicted the church of St. Cattwg in Gelligaer, the ancient parish of which formed the Council's area. Later that year the spelling of the Council's name was corrected.

In 1949 it was decided to expand the double-deck fleet. Two AEC Regent IIIs came in the summer of that year with bodywork constructed locally by Bruce Coachworks of Cardiff on East Lancs frames. These handsome vehicles were put to work on the Rhymney Bridge-Ystrad Mynach and Bargoed-Blackwood services: the other routes were unsuitable for double-deckers.

In 1950 the trend towards AEC was confirmed with the purchase of four new Regal III vehicles, all with Duple bus bodies featuring polished beading. They were used mainly on the services to Bedlinog from Pontypridd and from Bargoed. As with other arrivals at this time, the fleet numbers were allotted by gap filling and did not run in order: these four were given numbers 11, 17, 20 and 21. However, in 1951 the Council returned to Leyland and took delivery of four more Leyland PS1/1 models with Duple bodywork similar to that on the AECs supplied the previous year. The order had been placed in 1948, well in advance, and initially the vehicles were not expected until 1953: this was done because of the problems which had been experienced in the immediate post-war period, but the Council had failed to appreciate that the very heavy demand for new buses which existed in 1945-50 was coming to an end, and so Leyland were able to supply the vehicles two years earlier than expected.

With effect from 1st April 1950 the old Williamson tickets were abandoned in favour of a Bell Punch system known as Bellgraphic.

By 1951 many operators were turning away from half-cab, vertical-engined vehicles and were taking delivery of underfloor-engined single-deckers, which afforded increased seating capacity and in the long term one-man operation. The changeover to such single-deckers was almost universal across the country and happened very speedily in 1950-1: it was far more widespread and more expeditious than the retreat from forward-engined double-deckers was to be in the early 1960s. However, there were very few operators which continued with the older models, which in any event were still being constructed for overseas markets. Gelligaer was the only such municipal operator in Wales (apart from the special needs of the West Mon Board in relation to buses for Bargoed Hill): the best known in England was probably the Burnley Colne & Nelson Joint Transport Committee, some of whose more rural routes had poor operating conditions with which to contend, as did Gelligaer. In November 1950 a Sentinel underfloor-engined vehicle was demonstrated, but no orders resulted.

Route developments between 1945 and 1968, when there were major innovations, were modest, although soon after the end of the war frequencies were restored to at least those which had been in existence prior to hostilities. The Bargoed-Fochriw service was improved to hourly during some parts of the day, although there were additional journeys to Deri, which was regarded as a separate service, and the Bargoed-Ystrad Mynach via Gelligaer service was run every hour instead of two hourly. Some additional journeys were introduced on the Bargoed-Ystrad Mynach via Cefn Hengoed route, but they ran via Graig Hengoed instead of Hengoed Avenue and Brynavon Terrace.

The Fochriw service was extended in November 1945 down a steep and narrow road to terminate at Pontlottyn, on the main road, where there was a railway station and a magistrates' court as well as shops. In 1954 there was a proposal to improve frequencies on this service, which was resisted by British Rail, predictably but on entirely spurious grounds. In fact, the Council was granted permission with effect from 17th January 1955 to divert into the NCB housing estate at Fochriw, which necessitated negotiating some difficult roads with poor surfaces and required a diversion shortly thereafter and, subsequently, one way running round the houses.

On 16th February 1948 the Bargoed-Bedlinog service was extended from Bedlinog Square up a very steep hill to George Street, the terminus being known as the Coal Yard, serving a higher part of the village. It was agreed from the commencement of the service that there should be no stops on the hill, and shortly after it began one of the drivers suggested a device be fitted to prevent run-backs. However, the Traffic Commissioner had imposed no special conditions on it in relation to vehicles or equipment. When the service was duplicated, the extra usually terminated at the Square and the Manager asserted on a number of occasions that

only three buses were properly equipped to run up the very steep gradient, these being from the 1950 batch of AEC Regals. It was not until June 1969 that it was agreed to introduce an intermediate stop at Bedlinog bridge. The Pontypridd service by contrast ran to Hylton Terrace, Bedlinog, also beyond the Square but not requiring the climb.

There was a minor rerouting on the Blackwood service after the war to avoid a low bridge at Fleur de Lis, which enabled double-deckers to be used by both the joint operators, and from September 1949 the frequency on the route was improved from hourly to every thirty minutes. However, in November 1956 the route was altered to its previous line and in consequence single-deckers only could be used, although there are records of double-deckers running thereafter, perhaps on the modified route. In December 1959 this service was diverted via Lewis Lewis Avenue, Blackwood, to serve new housing. The road acquired its unusual repetitious name from that of a former chairman of the West Mon Board.

In 1946 the possibility of extending the Rhymney Bridge service to Dowlais Top was explored with Merthyr but it was eventually decided that an application for such a service would not succeed, because the road was already covered by Red & White. In 1948 the growth of the Heolddu housing estate led to an increased service with effect from 10th May of that year, and then to a route variation with effect from 30th January 1949 via the extension of St Gwladys Avenue, Heolddu Grove and Heolddu Crescent, to achieve greater penetration of the estate.

In September 1948, it was resolved to start running to Gelligaer Hospital. This, the Council's most obscure stage service, began running on Wednesdays and Saturdays only from 18th January 1950: it commenced at Penpedairheol, between Pengam and Gelligaer, and ran a short distance north along Hospital Road and then along a lane to the Hospital itself.

There was also an interesting development with the main road service to Rhymney Bridge. To the west of Rhymney, but within the Gelligaer area, was a small and isolated settlement named Bute Town, which had been constructed in the early nineteenth century to house workers from the Union Iron Company, with which the Bute family later became associated. Alternate northbound buses were diverted to serve Bute

One of the AEC Regal/Duples, No. 17, later 2 and here temporarily 52, is seen as late as 1967, shortly before withdrawal, at Tiryberth. The body was rebuilt by Longwell Green in 1958/9 and the outsweep of the skirt removed.

The third of the 1950 delivery of Regals was No. 20, later 3, seen at Bargoed on the local service in 1961, after being rebuilt.

Town, but returned from Rhymney Bridge via the usual route through Penydre. A passenger from Bute Town could only, therefore, travel south by staying on the bus at the terminus and coming back down into Rhymney. This began, after much consideration, on 22nd September 1952. It had first been considered in 1949, and there was further talk of cooperation with Merthyr Corporation on a through route, and then problems with Red & White, who were sceptical about the diversion. In November 1956 the Council was asked to provide services to the Ty Coch, Penydre and Tanybryn estates, in Rhymney, but said this was not possible, not least as it was out of their area: no such services were subsequently introduced by any operator.

Some members of the Transport Committee were expansionist in nature, and did not appear to comprehend the licensing difficulties which faced any application for new routes. There were occasional calls for many years (even as late as 1968) for through services from Rhymney Bridge to Cardiff, rather than using the connections which were made at Ystrad Mynach. The only substantial extension, which was temporary, was that the main road service ran hourly to Caerphilly between 7th and 12th August 1950, to allow residents to visit the annual National Eisteddfod.

The most pressing need of the Council was for a new depot. Those who lived near the existing premises in Aeron Place, Gilfach, constantly complained about the nuisance caused by the buses, particularly as numbers expanded and double-deckers entered the fleet. The project was much delayed by the war and thereafter by the need for building permits and the like. The Transport Committee, ever optimistic, agreed to the purchase of the new double-deckers in 1949 on the basis that the new garage would be open by then. However, although the site at Tiryberth, on the New Road between Pengam and Hengoed, had been definitively agreed in 1946, it was not until 1952 when the new garage and offices were opened, at a cost of £46,000, far more than would have been the case before the war. There had been a ceremony in 1951 at which the Chairmen of the Council and of the Transport Committee had cut the first sod: there was then an official opening, on 3rd July 1952. In fact, as late as 1946 an estimate of £16,000 had been given, which was then revised within three years to £50,000, but on the

basis that 40 buses could be housed, which was far more than were required: it was then reduced accordingly, on the understanding that the garage could be extended as required but would initially house 30. The new premises were situated centrally so far as the operations were concerned, and there was at last space to accommodate the still increasing fleet. Immersion heaters for the radiators were installed but were not to prove satisfactory in operation. In September 1955 it was agreed to install saloon heaters in all buses and a programme was put into effect over the next few years.

The opening of the new garage was a suitable prelude to the marking of the 25th anniversary of the commencement of operation, which was celebrated in 1953.

In 1953 there was a reorganisation of the former Jones Brothers services, following a meeting between the municipalities and Red & White on 30th April 1953. There was further integration with Red & White, and the new pattern allowed for some double-deck operation on the Pontypridd-Blackwood service by rerouting it so as to avoid a low bridge between Treharris and Trelewis: the Blackwood service, therefore, became more direct, running straight to Nelson from Pontypridd. The Pontypridd-Nelson-Bedlinog (George Street) direct service was thereafter run entirely by Red & White, every two hours, alternating with their Pontypridd-Nelson-Gelligaer-Bargoed service, and a new Pontypridd-Treharris-Nelson-Bedlinog (Hylton Terrace) service was run hourly, alternately by Red & White and the joint municipalities: this involved a double run into Nelson, which in about 1956 was provided with a small bus station. There were additional Pontypridd-Treharris short journeys, which ran only on Saturdays and were run alternate weeks by Red & White and by the municipalities.

As a consequence of this new cooperation, Red & White showed the Gelligaer sections between Bargoed and Nelson and between Nelson and Bedlinog (George Street) on the same tables as their respective services, while still ignoring completely the municipal operations between Bargoed and Rhymney Bridge, over which they both ran on a coordinated timetable.

From 18th January 1954 there was a further revision to the Pontypridd-Bedlinog service which involved the diversion of only those journeys run

In 1953 the Council took delivery of another double-decker, No. 3, later 9 (MTG 620), which was to run more than a million miles in service: here it is at Ystrad Mynach, about to return yet again to Rhymney Bridge, making connection with a West Mon vehicle on the Cardiff-Tredegar service.

One of the very last half-cab single-deckers delivered to the Council was No. 15, later 13, (OTG 321), which arrived as late as October 1954. It shows its classic lines at Tiryberth depot in October 1967.

by the joint municipal operators into Taff Merthyr Garden Village, between Trelewis and Bedlinog, which had been built as a small suburb for the mine of that name. This had been proposed as early as 1949, but until road improvements were carried out even the Bedford OWBs found the turns in the Village too tight. In the austere climate of the time, the Minister initially refused to consent to the work to the roads being carried out and Red & White categorically refused on many occasions to run round the diversion. This so exasperated the Council that it was resolved to display notices condemning the attitude of the company.

Many of the services to Bedlinog required duplication at this time, especially on Saturdays. The local councillor, Mr DB Cooke, was constantly pressing for extensions and improvements, and in 1954 wanted the two termini in the village linked by a loop, something which was only achieved very many years later. The residents then unsuccessfully called for an extension from George Street to Pleasant View. Bedlinog had been a centre of political activism since bitter union strife over the Taff Merthyr Colliery in the 1930s and there was a strong Communist element in the village.

Councillor Cooke also raised the suggestion of running from Bedlinog to Bargoed via Deri, which would have involved travelling across the so-called "Mountain Road" east of Bedlinog. This was not a development welcomed by the Transport Manager, and in both 1954 and 1956 trials took place over that route in which members of the Committee took part: both showed that apart from negligible traffic potential the roads were unsuitable for bus operation. In September 1958 there were complaints that on occasion buses could not negotiate the hill at Bedlinog, so passengers at the George Street terminus were left waiting. In June 1959 the Manager was asked to report on a proposal to use a converted van to connect outlying farms, and, yet again, of operating a service via the mountain road to Bargoed: these suggestions were predictably given no encouragement.

There was also, at this time, an increase in the number of journeys between Bargoed and Ystrad Mynach via Graig Hengoed, so that there was largely an hourly service via that route and an hourly service on the original route. The labyrinthine structure of the Council's administration meant that the recommendation to that effect came from the Hengoed Ward subcommittee as long before its implementation as 1950. During the Suez emergency the shortage of fuel caused some reduction on this route and on the alternative route via Gelligaer for a time, and services were not fully restored: for an experimental period in 1957 one journey each way was diverted to serve parts of both Hengoed routes. However, one important recommendation, in October 1958, for the construction of an off-road bus station at Bargoed, was never taken forward and the unsatisfactory triangle terminus continued to be used.

In 1953 the Council received more new vehicles. The double-deck fleet was increased to five by the delivery of Leyland PD2/10 MTG 620 in February. It was fitted with Leyland's own lowbridge bodywork and used almost exclusively on the long Rhymney Bridge-Ystrad Mynach service. It was to prove a particularly sturdy vehicle from a marque then known for its durability, and when withdrawn in 1971 had run over one million miles, mostly up and down the same valley roads.

The other two deliveries that year were more unconventional, in that they were on AEC Regal III chassis, which by then was widely regarded as obsolete, with half-cab forward-entrance bodies constructed by Longwell Green, which took its name from the village outside Bristol, on Park Royal frames. Longwell Green was to become the regular supplier of bodywork to Gelligaer over the next few years. It was a relatively small constructor, but developed a niche market in South Wales, which was not far from its base, with a particular emphasis towards the municipal market.

In 1954 the final two half-cabs arrived, which were among the last to that design delivered in this country. They were also AEC Regal IIIs with Longwell Green bodies and marked the end of an era. However, even then the Council were anxious to proceed with further similar vehicles: the minutes of the Transport Committee, which contain a great deal of trivia, give no indication of why this viewpoint continued. However, in January 1955 it was reported that AEC could not supply a further two Regals for at the least six months, and Leyland were not prepared to be any more accommodating in relation to Tigers. It was only this reluctance on the part of the

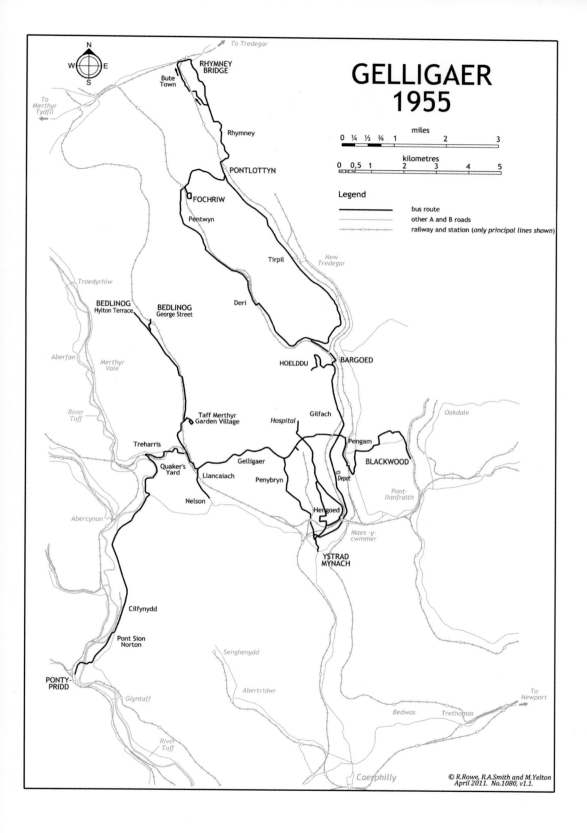

GELLIGAER 1955

To Tredegar

RHYMNEY BRIDGE
Bute Town
Rhymney
PONTLOTTYN
FOCHRIW
Pentwyn
Tirpil
New Tredegar
Deri
BEDLINOG Hylton Terrace
BEDLINOG George Street
Troedyrhiw
Aberfan
Merthyr Vale
River Taff
HOELDDU
BARGOED
Taff Merthyr Garden Village
Hospital
Gilfach
Oakdale
Treharris
Pengam
BLACKWOOD
Quaker's Yard
Gelligaer
Depot
Pont-llanfraith
Llancaiach
Penybryn
Nelson
Hengoed
Abercynon
Maes-y-cwmmer
YSTRAD MYNACH
Cilfynydd
Senghenydd
Pont Sion Norton
PONTY-PRIDD
Glyntaff
Abertridwr
To Newport
Bedwas
Trethomas
River Taff
Caerphilly

miles
0 ¼ ½ ¾ 1   2   3

kilometres
0 0,5 1   2   3   4   5

Legend

━━━━━━ bus route
∙∙∙∙∙∙∙ other A and B roads
┼┼┼┼┼┼ railway and station (only principal lines shown)

To Merthyr Tydfil

© R.Rowe, R.A.Smith and M.Yelton
April 2011. No.1080, v1.1.

29

manufacturers which finally convinced Gelligaer to have underfloor-engined vehicles demonstrated, in March 1955, and then to order two.

It was in those circumstances the first two underfloor-engined vehicles, RTX 965/6, which were also the first eight feet wide vehicles in the fleet, arrived later in 1955. They were AEC Reliances with Longwell Green 44-seat bodies which, unusually, featured an offside driver's door for access to the cab, at the insistence of Gelligaer, which required a fully enclosed area for the driver. The increase in capacity was noteworthy and welcome during rush hours: most of the Gelligaer routes ran only half hourly or hourly, so it was important to take up all the passengers who were waiting for a particular journey. There was no real difference in cost between the Reliances and what would have been paid for Regals.

In 1957 the Council took delivery of two further AEC Reliances with Longwell Green bodies, which in due course were to be converted for one-man operation when that was eventually introduced. A further two followed in 1958.

In 1959 another double-decker arrived. 359 CTX was a Leyland PD2/40 with a Longwell Green lowbridge body and power-operated platform doors, which was also used on the main road service. It was followed the next year by 751 HNY, to the same specifications and indeed the same order covered both vehicles. They were to be the last double-deckers to be bought until 1971. Longwell Green double-deck bodies were unusual but these were less distinctive than some: they did not feature the curved line above the front of the cab, as was found on those supplied to Newport and elsewhere.

The fleet had been completely refurbished since the war and also increased in numbers as frequencies were improved. In early 1960 the Transport Manager attended a demonstration of the Guy Wulfrunian in Cardiff: perhaps fortunately for the future of the undertaking, no order for one of those ill-starred vehicles followed.

However, by this time the decline in numbers was becoming very clear, here as elsewhere. In 1960 it was recorded that the number of passengers had fallen by 17% over 5 years. In 1950 about £6,000 per month was being taken in fares, and in April 1956 the amount exceeded £10,000 for the first time, but this was only achieved because fares were being increased as expenses soared.

In 1956 the tickets issued were about 400,000 per month, and this remained stationary for some years, but then began falling away and in 1963 fell beneath 300,000 per month, although at that stage the receipts had only just moved the accounts into deficit. By 1959 it had become apparent that there were serious problems with the receipts and running expenses on the former CMS services in particular.

It was resolved in late 1960 that for 1961 only one AEC Reliance be taken into stock, for financial reasons, although in 1962 and 1963 two arrived in each year, all with Longwell Green bodies. By the end of 1963 no fewer than 16 vehicles in a fleet then numbering 29 in total had bodywork by Longwell Green.

That dominance was, however, to cease, as Longwell Green were running out of customers for bus bodywork. Gelligaer provided their only orders in the 1961-3 period, and thereafter they built only two more buses, both in 1965, which were AEC Regent V models for Pontypridd, with the only front-entrance double-deck bodies constructed by the firm, so their days were numbered in this specialist field. In late 1964 Gelligaer enquired of Longwell Green about rebuilding work required for the first of the two double-deckers they had supplied, but in fact the work was carried out by Caerphilly UDC in 1966.

Initially, the decisions taken to contain losses were very conservative. In January 1961 it was resolved to curtail somewhat the service to Pontlottyn and in particular the short runs to Deri. In June 1961 it was decided to increase fares to bring in a further £6,300, which was the anticipated deficit, and by January 1962 financial stability had been re-established. The following year there was a small loss, but by January 1963 it was decided to consider each service and to see which reductions for economy could be made. That year saw a further reduction of 11% in traffic, but when the matter came back for consideration in July 1963, the only recommendation was to axe alternate services into Glyngaer, which was rejected by the Committee. Traffic increased marginally the next year.

In 1964 a further two AEC Reliances arrived at Gelligaer, but they carried Willowbrook bodies, as did a further two the following year.

In South Wales as elsewhere at this time there were extensive closures of railway lines, many of which either had or were thought to have

A novel single-decker, No. 28 later 15, (RTX 966) was one of two AEC Reliances with Longwell Green bodies and is at Bargoed in 1959, about to depart on the steep route through Cefn Hengoed.

By 1967, when Longwell Green-bodied Reliance No. 4 was seen at Gilfach on the Cefn Hengoed service, the AEC badge had been moved to the bottom of the front panel.

A second Leyland PD2/40 with Longwell Green bodywork followed in 1960 in the form of No. 14, later 23 (751 HNY), seen in 1967 working on its usual run to Ystrad Mynach via New Road.

In 1961 the Council, for financial reasons, bought only one new single-decker, a further AEC Reliance with Longwell Green body. 29, later 24, (363 MTG) is sitting outside the garage in the sun in 1969.

outlived their usefulness. One such was the line from Bargoed to Merthyr via Fochriw, which had never in any event carried much passenger traffic. In many places, rail replacement services were introduced, few of which lasted any length of time because they were not fashioned to connect with remaining services or to provide speedy and useful links. One was a service between Bargoed and Merthyr, introduced in 1963, jointly operated by the Council and by Red & White but financed by British Railways. It offered only one journey in each direction every day, and ran along the Bargoed-Deri-Pontlottyn route to Fochriw, then cut across some uninhabited countryside with a timing point at South Tunnel (Road Junction), before reaching Dowlais Top and then running on to Merthyr Railway Station. It was the only service to serve the very isolated settlement of Penywaun, on the moors and within Gelligaer. It was numbered 4 by Gelligaer, 163 by Red & White and was predictably short lived in operation, ending, as with so many such services, after the expiry of its three year introductory period. It ceased on 4th July 1966 after BR withdrew its funding save for one return journey on Saturdays: that lasted until 3rd December 1971 before ceasing also. The introduction of the service had again provoked controversy as Gelligaer thought they should run it on their own account, without Red & White, and, in any event, Merthyr objected to both of them commencing a new service. In due course, and after the introduction of the joint service, Merthyr began running to Cwm Bargoed and in 1965 Gelligaer, by then appreciating the limited traffic potential of the area, invited them to extend their service to Fochriw on Saturday rather than running a service themselves. Merthyr agreed provided Gelligaer subsidised it and it ran from 1st January 1966 for a period, but was also not remunerative.

In 1965 the hospital service was discontinued in the light of the small numbers using it: predictably, by early 1966 some members of the Transport Committee pressed for its reintroduction, but they were not successful.

In 1964 and then throughout most of 1965, Mr Collins was ill and off work. As a result, in February 1966 JA Edwards, the chief traffic clerk, was appointed as temporary manager and the full time position was advertised. Shortly thereafter it was filled when Roy Marshall arrived as general manager. He was a long-standing enthusiast as well as having a great deal of experience in the municipal sector, lastly as traffic superintendent in Southport. He was to stay for five years before moving on, and those years were to see extremely significant changes in the way in which the undertaking ran its operations. As with other adjoining local authorities, time had stood still in Gelligaer for a number of years and one-man operation, which was practicable on a number of the routes, had not been introduced. The economics had changed over the years so that running a 35-seater bus with a crew of two was no longer a practical proposition. The ground for the introduction of modernisation had been laid already, as single-manning had been first discussed in July 1965, and a visit had been arranged to nearby Aberdare, which had adopted this system. In January 1966 the union had agreed in principle (although the next few years saw many difficulties with its members on this issue) and on 1st March 1966 the full Council resolved to proceed in that direction.

When the new general manager came to South Wales, he inherited a fleet of 30, comprising the three Leyland double-deckers, 12 half-cab single-deckers of Leyland or AEC manufacture, and 15 AEC Reliances of various ages. One of his first steps was to renumber the fleet in order of age, so that vehicles of the same vintage were numbered consecutively rather than at random. This was done in July 1966.

In late 1966 two further Reliances arrived also with Willowbrook bodies but with dual-entrances and power-operated doors. They were equipped with BET style destination displays, which allowed the display of another innovation, the general introduction of route numbers. The date of these being allocated is not clear, but they came into general use at this time. The basic scheme was as follows:

1. Rhymney Bridge-Pontlottyn-Bargoed-Ystrad Mynach.
1A. As 1 but travelling north via Bute Town.
2. Bargoed-Gelligaer-Ystrad Mynach.
3. Bargoed-Gelligaer-Nelson-Bedlinog (George Street).
4. Bargoed-Blackwood.
5. Bargoed-Cefn Hengoed-Ystrad Mynach.
5A. Bargoed-Cefn Hengoed-Graig Hengoed-Ystrad Mynach.
6. Bargoed-Heolddu.

7/8. Bargoed-Deri-Fochriw-Pontlottyn.
185.(Red & White number). Pontypridd-
 Treharris-Nelson-Bedlinog (Hylton
 Terrace).

The new emphasis on publicity meant that instead of the Council's own timetables, which had been issued periodically for local circulation but which were not often seen outside the immediate area, the services as revised in March 1967 were included in the joint Red & White/Western Welsh timetable for the Eastern Valleys, issued on 4th June 1967. That itself marked an important landmark, because as the heavy traffic of the preceding twenty years began to fall off, the two major local company operators found themselves with intertwined networks and too many depots, whereas by combining their route patterns they were each able to reduce mileage and close some garages. Nearly all the services previously licensed to one or other of the companies were thereafter nominally joint: these included the long established Bargoed-Pontlottyn-Rhymney Bridge service of Red & White and the through Newport-Bedwas-Caerphilly-Ystrad Mynach-Bargoed service of Western Welsh. At that time also, Bedwas & Machen UDC, which had previously run only the alternate short journeys on that service from Newport to Caerphilly, began running all the way though on some timings.

As part of the general reorganisation, Red & White abandoned their Pontypridd-Nelson-Bargoed or Bedlinog services (then numbered 180 and 182 respectively) but continued operating the Pontypridd-Treharris-Nelson-Bedlinog service jointly with Gelligaer, but without any involvement from Western Welsh.

The 180 and 182 were later reinstated for a time, but in due course and after Bedlinog was taken from the new Rhymney Valley District Council, Bedlinog was linked to Merthyr, to which it had never had a direct service, and the municipal service from Bargoed was curtailed at Nelson.

Many journeys on the Bargoed-Ystrad Mynach via Hengoed services were extended to the Royal Oak as had been the old service 1, and alternate services on the Bargoed-Ystrad Mynach via Gelligaer service were diverted via the Greenhill Estate in Gelligaer, running along Aneurin Bevan Avenue, named after the local political hero. This was introduced from 31st March 1969, initially in the afternoons only and those journeys no longer ran the short double run via Glyngaer, in order to ensure that timings were kept. This diversion had been under consideration since 1959, and was again raised in 1963, but was not entirely popular with the union, which was worried about pressure on timings.

Following the arrival of the two Reliances, the new manager then had the undertaking buy two more of the same model, but this time they were second hand and had previously run with local independent Jones of Aberbeeg. A third was bought for spares only. One of the two thus acquired, TJU 686, was a former demonstrator for Duple Midland, which had built the body, although the front was later rebuilt after an accident. The other, UJU 774, had been a demonstrator for Willowbrook.

Roy Marshall was also anxious to test 36 feet long vehicles on the undertaking's routes, some of which ran along twisting and narrow roads. In late 1966 Gelligaer took a long Reliance on loan from South Wales Transport, together with a rear-engined AEC Swift and a Leyland Panther Cub, each from their respective manufacturers. The consequence was that the Swift, FGW 498C, which had a Willowbrook body seating 53, a similar number to the double-deckers, was acquired in April 1967 and converted to one-man operation, before entering service the following month. It had fluorescent lighting and air operated doors, both firsts for the fleet. It was followed in May 1967 by STB 957C, a Leyland Panther (a longer version of that used the previous year) but another former demonstrator, also bodied by Willowbrook. AEC agreed to sell the ex-demonstrator Swift for £4,800 only, which was a very competitive price.

One-man operation was now a high priority and was introduced gradually, commencing with the Bedlinog routes for which Setright ticket machines were acquired from Macbraynes. The older vehicles did not have power-operated doors and had to be converted so that the driver could operate the doors manually through a handle in the cab. On 19th September 1967 it was reported to the Committee that four shifts were one-man operated (for schools, factories and the like) and it was expected that this system be introduced on the ex-CMS service, which was the least lucrative of those run. As late as 1965/6 it was

In 1963 the last two vehicles constructed for the Council by Longwell Green were delivered. No. 23, later 28, (890 UTG). By September 1973 28 had been repainted in the new livery and was about to leave Bargoed for Pontlottyn.

In 1966 Gelligaer acquired two second-hand Reliances from Jones of Aberbeeg. No. 20 (TJU 686) was originally a Duple demonstrator and was fitted with a Duple Midland B44F body. In October 1967 it was at Gilfach bound for Bedlinog.

reported that losses were only being incurred on the two Bedlinog services and on Bargoed-Pontottyn via Deri and Fochriw. In late 1967 the undertaking was affected by industrial action, which reduced the receipts, and finally, on 13th February 1968, it was resolved to start one-man operation on the former CMS services with effect from 25th February 1968, whether or not the other participants agreed so to do. This duly occurred, and encompassed the Bargoed-Bedlinog service as well as most of the school, factory and colliery services which were not already so operated. An earlier suggestion to reduce the Bargoed-Bedlinog service to two hourly on Sundays was rejected by the Committee, one of the few occasions when they did not agree with successive Transport Managers: it was then suggested that timings would be assisted if the Taff Merthyr diversion were run off the Pontypridd rather than the Bargoed service, but that was never implemented. At that time, numbers seem to have stabilised for a time at about 275,000 per month.

The Bargoed town service was one of the first to come under Roy Marshall's scrutiny: on 15th November 1966 he suggested that it be converted to one-man operation, that any through journeys to Ystrad Mynach via the New Road be curtailed, and that it be rerouted in a circle back via Moorland Road to avoid having to reverse at the outer terminus. However, in June 1968 it was resolved that as a result of new housing being constructed at Gilfach, to the south of the existing route, application be made to run in a unidirectional loop along the perimeter of the new estate and back to Bargoed Town Centre via Western Drive and Hillside Park. It was also diverted off Heolddu Crescent because of problems with parked cars blocking the narrow residential streets. This longer route began on 20th October 1968.

As prosperity grew problems with parked cars also led to the Graig Hengoed service running along the main road rather than through Ash Grove, Acacia Avenue and Beech Drive, with effect from 4th January 1970. It had been traditional in South Wales to try and serve housing by penetration right into the estates, not least because of the gradients which were sometimes meant passengers walking from the main road, but this policy became more difficult as the years passed.

Roy Marshall later recorded his recollections of his time at Gelligaer, and made the point that the relatively small size of the undertaking made in some ways for efficiency, not least because the manager had his finger on the pulse with such a small staff. He discovered that the existing arrangements in force at the time he took over, which involved a crew usually keeping its own bus had worked well. One problem was that the second bus on the Blackwood service worked mornings one week, afternoons the next, and West Mon as joint operators corresponded. This led him to devise a plan for additional maintenance work which could be fitted round these workings.

Because of the small number of drivers, the undertaking ran with only one crew (later one man) on standby: absenteeism was rare, but if necessary an inspector, the depot foreman, or anyone else with a licence, would take on a driving duty if required. There were three inspectors employed by this time, one on mornings, one on afternoons and one as Traffic Superintendent, who dealt with scheduling and covered on the days off of the other two. A tyre fitter was shared with Caerphilly, and there were four other fitters, a painter, a coachbuilder and an apprentice. The painter then retired and spray painting was introduced for what was a fairly complicated livery. There was no heating at the depot, but there was the radiator immersion heating system to which vehicles were coupled up, but this was discontinued as unreliable and sometimes dangerous. The variety of tasks available made for a more interesting working life for the staff.

In addition to the garage staff, there were four employees in the office, reduced to three after the earlier Bellgraphic ticketing system was completely replaced by Setright machines.

Another new initiative at that time was to change the livery. In 1967 a number of vehicles were painted in red, with white window surrounds and dark green roof, restoring the pre-war colours, albeit applying them differently. However, in 1968 this was changed so that the white area came down almost as far as the wheel arches, and the red area was correspondingly reduced. This last version was first applied to two further AEC Swifts with Willowbrook dual-entrance bodywork which entered service at the end of 1968. A special livery was applied to the ex-demonstrator Swift in 1969 to mark the investiture of Prince Charles as Prince of Wales. The Manager's enthusiast credentials

AEC Swift No. 35 (FGW 498C) with Willowbrook B53F body. It is in its pre-investiture livery and is seen outside the garage on New Road in 1967.

Dual-entrance Willowbrook-bodied AEC Swift, No. 37 (TTX 37G) is seen here at Pengam in 1969 en route for Ystrad Mynach.

were also demonstrated when the Omnibus Society visited Gelligaer, on 29th June 1969.

The only other vehicle which was delivered in 1968 was an Austin van which the Council had fitted with windows and 11 perimeter seats, an unusual vehicle to be found in municipal ownership. The arrival of the rear-engined single-deckers enabled the fleet to be reduced from 30 to 27, as the increased capacity meant that they could cover school duties and the like which had previously required two smaller buses and the last half-cab single-deckers were withdrawn.

The major change in 1968, however, was to the long-established service pattern, which, apart from the Pontypridd route, had seen the Council's services largely confined to their own area and without access to the large conurbations to the south. All this was to change. There was a comprehensive rescheduling and relinking of services in August 1968 to incorporate the existing Western Welsh/Red & White/Bedwas & Machen service from Newport to Bargoed, the Western Welsh/Red & White service from Bargoed to Rhymney Bridge and Gelligaer services 1/1A from Ystrad Mynach to Rhymney Bridge. The new services were numbered 149 and 150: the 149 ran Newport-Bedwas-Caerphilly-Ystrad Mynach-Bargoed-Pontlottyn-Rhymney Bridge-Tredegar on an hourly headway, and the 150 shared its route as far as Rhymney Bridge and then went to Merthyr. Although that was the basic pattern, it was still necessary to change at Rhymney Bridge on many journeys to Tredegar or Merthyr, as the municipal operators ran only that far: local authority operation right through had to wait until Rhymney Valley DC came into existence. The Bute Town journeys continued in operation, although from 6th January 1969 the diversion ran only two hourly instead of hourly.

There were obvious benefits to the travelling public in this new arrangement, as many more direct journeys were available and access to Cardiff was also improved, by connection to train or bus at Caerphilly. It also meant that the buses of the two small municipalities involved were seen over a much wider area than before. Caerphilly was not involved, as for historical reasons they had never been participants in the Newport service. Predictably, it led to some councillors again enquiring why through routes were being run to Newport instead of the larger and more important

centre of Cardiff, but that was a consequence of the history of services in the area, and the new connections by train made the capital far more accessible.

This development and its consequences were of great importance in the history of the undertaking. Prior to its implementation, even the local Labour Party, staunch supporters of municipal transport, had begun to question whether the enterprise should be sold off. However, the reduction in frequency of buses along the Rhymney Valley and through running to new destinations increased receipts per mile. By early 1969, the financial position of the undertaking had improved very considerably.

In 1968 both Pontypridd and Caerphilly withdrew from the pool arrangements for the former Jones Brothers services. This resulted in Gelligaer continuing to run the Pontypridd-Bedlinog route with Red & White, but without any of the additional journeys previously run by Pontypridd, and West Mon running the Pontypridd-Blackwood service on their own, at a reduced frequency: in due course it was rerouted to its original line through Treharris. Gelligaer had themselves earlier considered abandoning the ex-CMS route, but decided that they could still continue provided that one-man operation was introduced. The Blackwood-Pontypridd service still runs in 2011, but Bedlinog is now connected only to Merthyr, although the service loops around the two termini in the village, as suggested by the Councillor so many years before.

After further problems with the trade union, with effect from 7th June 1970 the services from Bargoed to Ystrad Mynach via Gelligaer and via Hengoed and from Bargoed to Pontlottyn via Deri were converted to one-man operation. By August of that year the department was able to say that it was fully staffed, at a time when many such undertakings were struggling to recruit drivers.

The reduction in the numbers in the fleet had a positive side, but also led to difficulties when adverse weather conditions prevailed. In November 1970 four vehicles were damaged in one morning peak period, including one which rolled down a hill after a head-on collision. That was in addition to the older of the two Longwell Green-bodied Titans, which had been rammed in the back the week before and was prematurely retired. The crisis was solved by loaning an AEC

One of Roy Marshall's many legacies to the fleet was an order for three Bristol VRs with Northern Counties bodies, which were required for the new through service to Newport. They were far larger than any vehicle which had been operated before. A few days after delivery in 1971 No. 39 (BTX 539J) was at Ystrad Mynach heading north for Rhymney Bridge.

Roy Marshall also ordered nine Bristol REs which revitalised the fleet. In 1973, the year after delivery, No. 42 (KTX 242L), one of the first batch, is seen approaching Rhymney Bridge, having run on the northwards-only diversion via Bute Town.

Swift from Nottingham Corporation, an AEC Bridgemaster from Western Welsh, and a variety of vehicles, including a 20-year-old Leyland Titan, from Caerphilly. Another Caerphilly Titan, dating from 1958 and with Massey lowbridge bodywork, was taken on rather longer term loan and in January 1971 was purchased as a replacement for the written-off Longwell Green Titan.

In 1970 Mr Edwards retired, and then towards the end of the year Roy Marshall was appointed as manager of the larger undertaking of Burton-on-Trent. His departure was postponed until February 1971, and Mr L Green, his deputy, took over on an interim basis until the arrival of his replacement, Mr CW Sampson, who was to be the last Transport Manager of the independent undertaking. He was left with a much improved legacy, not least because on 2nd June 1970 the Committee finally decided that it was for the manager to appoint platform staff and also to discipline such staff, without any involvement from councillors in the first instance.

There were very few changes to the route pattern in the last few years. With effect from 17th January 1971 the Sunday service from Pontypridd was operated alternately to each of the two Bedlinog termini. From 21st December 1972, for a trial period, all services, as opposed to alternate buses, from Bargoed to Ystrad Mynach via Gelligaer were diverted along Aneurin Bevan Avenue. In September 1973 it was proposed to increase frequencies on the Cefn Hengoed route as housing development was continuing on it.

Before he left Roy Marshall had persuaded the Council that, with the new route pattern, replacement double-deckers were required, but that it would be possible to reduce the size of the fleet. Three Bristol VRs were ordered in December 1968, but did not arrive until April 1971, just after his departure, and were fitted with Gardner six-cylinder engines and Northern Counties bodies seating 77. They were crew-operated. One of the reasons for their specification was that a five-speed gearbox was needed for the varying conditions encountered on the lengthy Newport service, which had some quite long rural stretches as well as steep gradients and urban sprawl. They were the first rear-engined double-deckers supplied to any of the smaller Welsh municipalities and marked a very significant change in purchasing policy. They were also the first double-deckers to be painted in the 1968 livery.

The other order which had been placed by the Council before Roy Marshall's departure was for six, later nine, Bristol RE rear-engined single-deckers with Gardner power units and Eastern Coach Works bodies, a tried and tested combination which was far more reliable than the earlier Swifts and Panther. It was intended that three arrive in 1972, three the following year, and three in 1974, the 1973 arrivals being those added after the order had first been placed. The first three arrived in September 1972 and became a familiar sight in the area, including taking duties to Newport.

Earlier that year Gelligaer had purchased from Caerphilly a second hand 1954 Massey-bodied Leyland Royal Tiger as a replacement for the Duple Midland-bodied AEC Reliance, although it lasted only a short time. They had also purchased an AEC Regent V with Park Royal body and two AEC Reliances with Willowbrook dual-purpose bodies, all previously run by Western Welsh. The double-decker was largely used for driver training, but the purpose behind the acquisition of the Reliances was to make inroads into the private hire market in an attempt to assist the finances of the undertaking, which were by then again under considerable strain. In 1971 there was a deficit of £10,000 on the year's operations.

The trend towards private hire work was continued in 1973, the last full year of the Council's existence. In May 1973 a Bedford YRQ with Duple 45-seat coach bodywork was taken into stock, in an all-over cream livery, but it was disposed of to dealers by the end of the year and replaced by a Bedford YRT with Duple 53-seat coach bodywork, but which was capable of being used on bus services, as a condition of the grant used to purchase it. It carried a white livery with a pale blue flash. More conventional deliveries, in October 1973, were the further three Bristol RE vehicles, this time fitted with ECW bodies but to dual-purpose rather than bus standards: they formed the additional batch of vehicles pre-ordered. They were painted in yet another new livery, which was predominantly white but had a pale green skirt and a red band beneath the windows. The first of these, numbered 45, was seriously damaged very early in its service and was rebuilt in January 1974 by Red & White with an all red front.

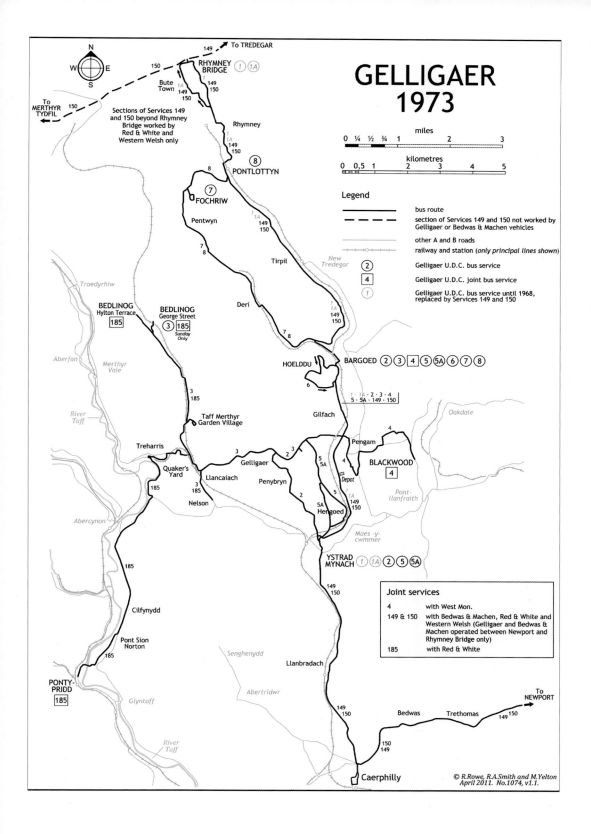

GELLIGAER 1973

miles

0 ¼ ½ ¾ 1   2   3

kilometres

0   0,5   1   2   3   4   5

Legend

————	bus route
– – – –	section of Services 149 and 150 not worked by Gelligaer or Bedwas & Machen vehicles
————	other A and B roads
——+——+——	railway and station (only principal lines shown)
②	Gelligaer U.D.C. bus service
④	Gelligaer U.D.C. joint bus service
①	Gelligaer U.D.C. bus service until 1968, replaced by Services 149 and 150

Sections of Services 149 and 150 beyond Rhymney Bridge worked by Red & White and Western Welsh only

To TREDEGAR

RHYMNEY BRIDGE ① 1A

Bute Town

Rhymney

⑧ PONTLOTTYN

⑦ FOCHRIW

Pentwyn

Tirpil

New Tredegar

Deri

Troedyrhiw

Aberfan

Merthyr Vale

BEDLINOG Hylton Terrace ③ 185

BEDLINOG George Street ③ 185 Sunday Only

River Taff

HOELDDU

BARGOED ② ③ ④ ⑤ 5A ⑥ ⑦ ⑧

1 · 1A · 2 · 3 · 4 5 · 5A · 149 · 150

Taff Merthyr Garden Village

Gilfach

Oakdale

Treharris

Quaker's Yard

Gelligaer

Llancaiach

Penybryn

Pengam

BLACKWOOD ④

Depot

Pont-llanfraith

Nelson

Hengoed

Maes-y-cwmmer

Abercynon

YSTRAD MYNACH ① 1A ② ⑤ 5A

Cilfynydd

Senghenydd

Pont Sion Norton

Llanbradach

PONTY-PRIDD 185

Glyntaff

Abertridwr

River Taff

Bedwas

Trethomas

To NEWPORT

Caerphilly

Joint services

4	with West Mon.
149 & 150	with Bedwas & Machen, Red & White and Western Welsh (Gelligaer and Bedwas & Machen operated between Newport and Rhymney Bridge only)
185	with Red & White

© R.Rowe, R.A.Smith and M.Yelton
April 2011. No.1074, v1.1.

Continuing difficulties in 1973 saw the extensive hiring in of vehicles, from a variety of sources including Cardiff Corporation, which supplied a Guy Arab with highbridge body, and Caerphilly Corporation, which supplied two Leyland Titans with Massey lowbridge bodies. The following year saw the purchase of an AEC Regent V with Massey body from Bedwas & Machen: it continued to run in their livery, albeit with Gelligaer fleetnames and legal lettering. Another Regent from the same source was on loan for some time. In January 1974 one of the Gelligaer REs was exchanged for a fortnight with a single-deck Daimler Fleetline with Willowbrook body which had been purchased by Roy Marshall's new employers, Burton Corporation.

When the new arrangements for local government took effect, and Gelligaer was absorbed into the new Rhymney Valley District Council, which was essentially the fulfilment from a transport viewpoint of a policy which the old Council had supported for many years, there were three further Bristol REs on order, which were delivered direct to the new authority in January 1975. The Bristol marque had become in the last few years the mainstay of the Gelligaer undertaking.

Initially, Rhymney Valley continued the same services as its constituents had run, and retained the Caerphilly depot in Mill Road and the Gelligaer depot in Tiryberth: the small Bedwas & Machen garage was closed. In due course, however, deregulation went to the head of those running what became Inter Valley Link, and the organisation over-expanded and then financially collapsed. The Tiryberth premises were retained by the District Council for its service vehicles.

The second batch of Bristol REs arrived in 1973 and the three vehicles were all painted white, with green skirts and a red band below the windows. Number 46 (NKG 246M) was in Caerphilly in April 1974, just after the end of Gelligaer operation but still in full livery.

FLEET LIST

Fleet numbers were carried from the commencement of services in 1928, but were re-allocated as vehicles were withdrawn, so became scattered throughout batches. In July 1966 the entire fleet was renumbered in chronological order.

Information is set out below as follows:

FLEET NUMBER	1966 RENUMBER	REG'N NUMBER	CHASSIS	BODYWORK	SEATING

1928

1	-	TX 6324	Leyland TS2	Leyland	B29D
2	-	TX 6326	Leyland TS2	Leyland	B29D
3	-	TX 6367	Leyland TS2	Leyland	B29D
4	-	TX 6369	Leyland TS2	Leyland	B29D
5	-	TX 6459	Albion SPLB24	Hall, Lewis	B20F
6	-	TX 6460	Albion SPLB24	Hall, Lewis	B20F

Operations began with vehicles on loan, as described in the text, and the first vehicles owned by the Council were the four Leylands, which arrived in November 1928, followed the next month by two small Albions for the Bedlinog service. The first two Leylands and possibly the others were refitted with AEC engines in about 1933. 1 was withdrawn in 1936 and passed to Cardiff Corporation for spares: the other three Leylands stayed until 1939, with 2 seeing further service in South Wales and then passing to Primrose of Leominster after being re-bodied and lasting in service until 1951. 3 was used as an ambulance in the war and then ran for a private operator in Rhymney until 1948: 4 went to the Air Ministry. The two Albions were retained only until 1934 and both were sold to Scottish operators and re-bodied as lorries.

1929

9	-	NY 7501	AEC 202	United	B25D
8	-	NY 9178	AEC 202	United	B24D
7	-	TX 606	AEC 414	United	B26D
11	-	TX 2462	Lancia Pentaiota	Hall, Lewis6	B26
10	-	TX 6097	Thornycroft SB	Hall, Lewis	B26
9	-	TX 7748	Thornycroft A6	Northern Counties	B26

The Thornycroft A6 was purchased new and withdrawn as early as 1934. The three United-bodied AECs came from Matthews of Ystrad Mynach. They were already three or four years old on acquisition and 9 was almost immediately withdrawn: the other two lasted only until 1931. The Lancia and the Thornycroft SB came from Waters of Ystrad Mynach and were newer, dating from 1927 and 1928 respectively and staying until 1931 and 1932.

1931

7	-	TG 1152	AEC Regal	Metcalfe	B30D
8	-	TG 1154	AEC Regal	Metcalfe	B30D
11	-	TG 1339	AEC Regal	Metcalfe	B30D
12	-	TG 2590	AEC Regal	Weymann	B32D
13	-	TG 2599	AEC Regal	Weymann	B32D

The fleet was revitalised in 1931 with the acquisition of five AECs, two of which lasted until after the war. The exception was 8, which was taken out of service in 1933 and sold to Romilly Motors, the Cardiff dealers. This may have been as a result of an accident, and it was replaced by another Regal, it ran elsewhere for many years thereafter. The others were fitted with oil engines in 1935 and at about the same time were rebuilt to B32R with the front entrance being removed. 7 and 11 were withdrawn during the war, and 13 in 1947. The remaining vehicle, 12, was delicensed between 1947 and 1949 but was rebuilt during that time with a utility style finish, and remained in service until 1953. All the others save 12 also passed for further operations, but the last remaining vehicle became a coal merchant's office in Bedlinog.

Metcalfe-bodied AEC Regal No. 8 (TG 1154), delivered in 1931, is seen on trials at Bargoed.

There were two AEC Regals with Weymann bodies delivered in 1931. Here No. 13 (TG 2599) is seen at Hanbury Square, Bargoed with an unidentified vehicle passing.

1932

10		-	TG 3523	AEC Renown	Weymann	B38D

The arrival of this vehicle was a landmark. It was the first oil-engined vehicle to be operated by a South Wales municipality and all vehicles delivered to Gelligaer thereafter were so powered. It was also by far the most capacious vehicle operated to that date. It was altered to rear entrance only in 1934 and remained in the fleet until 1947.

Weymann-bodied AEC Renown delivered in 1932, is seen before conversion to rear-entrance only in 1934.

1933

8	-		TG 4475	AEC Regal	Weymann B32D	B32D

This vehicle took the number and the place of the Regal which was sold to Romilly Motors. It was fitted with perimeter seating in 1941 and withdrawn in 1950. It was presumably rebuilt to rear entrance only, like the others.

A single AEC Regal with Weymann dual-entrance body, No. 8 (TG 4475) arrived in 1933.

1934

6		-	TG6594	AEC Regal 4	Weymanm	B32R
5		-	TG 6595	AEC Regal 4	Weymann	B32R
9		-	TG 8266	AEC Q	Short	B39C

The arrival of the two AEC Regals in January 1934 was a clear continuation of the policy which had been in existence for the preceding few years. They lasted until 1945/6 and passed to dealers. However, in August 1934 one of the revolutionary AEC Q types arrived: it was overhauled by Romilly Motors in 1936 and scrapped after a relatively short life in 1942.

In 1934 Gelligaer took delivery of the first of its two AEC Q vehicles. This was fitted with a Short body with centre entrance. Note the unusual position of the front number plate.

1936

14		-	MV 295	AEC Regal 4	Short	B32F

This Regal was a former demonstrator for the manufacturers, and had a metal-framed body. An AEC had been on loan, certainly from late 1933 until 1935, and it may have been this vehicle. It lasted until being scrapped in 1946.

The second Q type, No. 1 (BTX 113), arrived in 1937 and had an attractive centre entrance body by Strachans, giving it a very different appearance to the earlier vehicle.

1937

1		-	BTX 113	AEC Q	Strachans	B39C

The second Q, which looked very different from the first, arrived in January 1937 and stayed until December 1950, when it went for scrap. In 1944 it was proposed to fit a new body, but in fact the Council itself substantially rebuilt it in utility style between November 1944 and March 1946. The seating capacity appears to have been reduced to 36. On 4th April 1949 the vehicle was seriously damaged when it collided with a wall at Cascade, near Pengam, and several passengers were injured. It did not run again after that.

1938

15		-	DNY 448	Leyland TS8	Strachans	B37F
16		-	DNY 449	Leyland TS8	Strachans	B37F

These vehicles, the first Leylands for ten years, were fitted from new with saloon heaters, a rare accessory at that time. 15 was badly damaged in an accident in late 1944 and was initially repaired temporarily: in 1949 Modern Vehicle Constructors of Caerphilly were asked to replace the body but in due course this was done by Burlingham, albeit not until 1950, not 1945 as usually previously recorded. There was a dispute over the cost of this. 16 was re-bodied by Burlingham in 1946. It has been said that the new bodies initially had wooden seats to a B36F configuration, later replaced by conventional upholstered versions and becoming B34F, but it seems unlikely that that applied to 15. They lasted until 1954 and 1956 respectively: 16 had been seriously damaged in an accident at Hengoed on 11th November 1952 and may not have run after that date.

In 1938 the Council took delivery of two Strachans-bodied Leyland TS8s. Number 15 (DNY 448) was badly damaged in 1944 and was rebodied by Burlingham in 1950. Here it rounds the apex of Hanbury Square, Bargoed, in 1952.

1939

2	-		DTX 652	AEC Regal	Strachans	B36R
4			ETG 77	Leyland TS8	Strachans	B36R

The Council split its orders in 1939, with one vehicle being taken from AEC and one later in the year from Leyland. A third order was cancelled because of the outbreak of the war. The AEC had its body rebuilt or replaced in late 1946 by Green of Merthyr Tydfil, becoming B34F, and in this form lasted until 1954, when it was exported to Yugoslavia: the Leyland was rebuilt in 1950 by Bruce Coachworks to B34F, so extensively that it was effectively rebuilt, and in this form it lasted until 1958, again passing for further service and then to a showman. The rebuilding followed an incident on 31st December 1949 when the vehicle was involved in a fatal accident when it collided with a motor cycle, but the Council's driver was exonerated.

In 1939 the Council bought one AEC and one Leyland, both with Strachans bodies. The AEC Regal, No. 2 (DTX 652) is shown here on delivery.

The Leyland delivered in 1939 was No. 4 (ETG 77) seen here in a drab Bargoed in 1949.

1943

17		-	FNY 171	Bedford OWB	Duple	B32F
9		-	FNY 172	Bedford OWB	Duple	B32F
3		-	FNY 173	Bedford OWB	Duple	B32F
18		-	FNY 457	Bedford OWB	Duple	B32F

After almost four years without new vehicles, four new utility Bedfords arrived, which were delivered in either dark grey (3, 9, 17) or chocolate (18) livery. All were later reseated to B30F and 18 was renumbered to 11 in 1944. The first withdrawal, 9, was in 1949, followed by 11, formerly 18, and 17 in 1950 and 3 in 1953. All were used by subsequent owners although they almost certainly did not have the heavy running which Gelligaer imposed on its vehicles.

The war brought an influx of Bedford OWBs, the small capacity of which meant they saw short service thereafter. However, No. 3 (FNY 173) was still in service in 1951 and was captured near the old depot in Aeron Place.

The year 1944 also saw the first double-deckers, two Daimlers with Brush lowbridge bodies. No. 14 (FNY 703) is outside the garage at Tiryberth on the Rhymney Bridge-Ystrad Mynach service upon which double-deckers were usually employed.

1944

18	-	FNY 559	Bedford OWB	Duple	B32F
19	-	FNY 612	Bedford OWB	Duple	B32F
14	-	FNY 703	Daimler CWA6	Brush	L27/28R
7	-	FNY 704	Daimler CWA6	Brush	L27/28R
20	-	FNY 875	Bedford OWB	Duple	B32F

A further three Bedford OWBs arrived the following year, all of which were also reseated to B30F like the first batch. They lasted only until 1949 (18), 1950 (20) or 1953 (19) but all ran subsequently. However, the innovation this year was the arrival of the first two double-deckers, which were employed almost exclusively on the long and heavily-trafficked Ystrad Mynach-Bargoed-Rhymney Bridge service, where the extra capacity was well used. As early as October 1951 they were in need of bodywork repairs and it was proposed to send them to Bruce Coachworks in Cardiff, but it was then found that that company was about to close, and they were repaired by Atlas Coachworks, also in Cardiff. In 1952 it was suggested that 14 be overhauled by Thomas Hoskin or Hosking of Cardiff (a former employee of Bruce), but that does not seem to have happened as in 1955 both were modernised by Longwell Green, by then the Council's preferred bodywork supplier. It was originally intended that Gelligaer themselves should rebuild 14, but in the event there was too much work on at the garage for the relatively small staff and it too was sent to Bristol. They lasted in that form until 1959 (7) and 1960 (14).

1945

21	-	HB 5985	Bedford OWB	Duple	B32F
22	-	YG 7448	Leyland TS6	Burlingham	B36F

The takeover of Jones Brothers of Treharris by the four municipal operators resulted in the sharing out between them of the fleet. Gelligaer received three vehicles, but one, WO 6575, a Dennis Lancet dating from 1931 with Weymann B31R body which may have been replaced in 1940, was not used by the Council. The Bedford OWB was new in 1943 and fitted in well with the existing fleet: it was reseated to B30F in company with the others and was kept only until 1950. The other acquisition, the Leyland, dated from 1934 and had been new to Ripponden & District with a Cravens B32F body. It passed to Jones Brothers in 1935 and was re-bodied in 1945, which explains why Gelligaer retained it after the takeover, together with the fact that it had an oil engine. It was reseated to 34 and remained in the fleet until 1956, eventually ending up with a showman.

On the takeover of Jones of Treharris in 1945 Gelligaer received two vehicles which would run, the newer of which was this Bedford OWB, No. 21 (HB 5985), seen in Bargoed in 1949.

The other vehicle acquired from Jones was this Leyland TS6 of 1934, which had been rebodied by Burlingham in 1945. It was at Bargoed on the Fochriw service, also in 1949.

1946

5		-	FTG 846	AEC Regal	Harrington	B36F
6		-	FTG 977	AEC Regal	Harrington	B36F
23		-	FTX 175	AEC Regal	Duple	DP35F

The first new vehicles delivered after the war started a trend towards conservative half-cab single-deckers which continued for a number of years. The two Harrington-bodied buses had utility style bodies and were reseated to 34 shortly after arrival. They stayed until 1958 and 1962 respectively, after being overhauled by Longwell Green in 1955. The Duple-bodied Regal was an unusual purchase as it had high-back coach type seats when new, which were later replaced by conventional bus seats. It was known as "the coach". It was kept until 1963, when, after an unsuccessful attempt to convert it for use as a snowplough, it was scrapped.

When Roy Marshall first visited the area, on 16th July 1949, he went first to Gelligaer village, where he photographed AEC Regal/Harrington No. 5 (FTG 846) en route to Bargoed from Bedlinog: he realised shortly after arriving that he was not at the hub of operations, and went on to Bargoed.

One of the AEC Regals with austere Harrington bodies delivered in 1946 was No. 6 (FTG 977), seen in 1952 in Bargoed against the background of a massive poster for the local cinema.

The third Regal which arrived in 1946 was much more unusual: it had a Duple body which originally had high-backed coach seats, later replaced as can be seen here in 1952 at Bargoed.

10		-	GTG 293	Leyland PS1/1	Willowbrook	B35F
13		-	GTG 294	Leyland PS1/1	Willowbrook	B35F
24		-	GTG 295	Leyland PS1/1	Willowbrook	B35F

In 1947 the suppliers of both chassis and body were changed, Willowbrook being engaged as a consequence of their promise to deliver speedily, but the use of half-cab single-deckers continued. These vehicles were all rebuilt by the Council in 1953-6 with rubber-mounted flush windows and were then reseated to 33. They were withdrawn in 1963 (10, which then became the Gelligaer UDC snowplough) and 1964 (13 and 24).

Three Leylands on PS1/1 chassis with Willowbrook bodies arrived in 1947. Number 10 (GTG293) is seen in Bargoed on Roy Marshall's first trip to the area, in 1949.

Increased loadings, particularly on the main road service from Rhymney Bridge to Ystrad Mynach, saw the acquisition in 1949 of two AEC Regents with handsome Bruce bodies. Number 9 (HTX 396) is on that service at Bargoed in 1951.

1949

9		-	HTX 396	AEC Regent III	Bruce	L27/26R
18		-	HTX 397	AEC Regent III	Bruce	L27/26R

The increased need for double-deckers saw the acquisition of two AEC Regents, which had Bruce bodies on East Lancs frames. They were used on the Ystrad Mynach to Rhymney Bridge service and also on the Bargoed to Blackwood route run jointly with West Mon, which was diverted in order to allow double-deckers to be used. The Board took delivery of two similar vehicles in the same year. In late 1962 18 was damaged in an accident and was rebuilt early the following year by the Council. They were both withdrawn and scrapped in 1965, and the decision was taken in advance to replace them with single-deckers.

1950

11	[1]	KNY 453	AEC Regal III	Duple	B35F
17	[2]	KNY 454	AEC Regal III	Duple	B35F
20	[3]	KNY 455	AEC Regal III	Duple	B35F
21	[4]	KNY 456	AEC Regal III	Duple	B35F

This year saw the arrival of four more Regals, which were fitted with Duple D style bodies with outswept skirts and a great deal of polished beading. They were used generally on the services to Bedlinog. In 1958/9 all four were rebuilt, 11 by the Council and the other three by Longwell Green, some losing the outsweep of the body at the skirt and all receiving rubber-mounted windows. During its rebuild in 1959, 17 was fitted for one-man operation. They were all withdrawn in 1966/7, 1[11] becoming a tyre store for the Council and 2[17] being used as a towing vehicle and for staff transport.

In 1951 a further four single-deckers arrived, but this time the chassis was by Leyland although the body was constructed by Duple and was similar to that provided the previous year. Number 26, later 6, (KNY 961) is seen at Bargoed early in its service.

1	[5]	KNY 960	Leyland PS1/1	Duple	B35F
26	[6]	KNY 961	Leyland PS1/1	Duple	B35F
8	[7]	KNY 962	Leyland PS1/1	Duple	B35F
25	[8]	KNY 963	Leyland PS1/1	Duple	B35F

The 1951 orders reverted to Leyland and arrived as many other operators were moving away from the traditional half-cab design in favour of underfloor-engined vehicles. The bodywork was similar to the AEC batch of the previous year and they were also rebuilt in 1956/7 by either the Council (1, 8 and 25) or by Longwell Green (26). They were used mostly on the back road services between Bargoed and Ystrad Mynach. They were withdrawn in 1966/7.

In 1956 No. 25, later 8, (KNY 963) was at Bargoed in a revised form of livery, having arrived from Pontlottyn via Fochriw and Deri, despite what the blind says!.

In 1968, No. 9 (MTG 620) was still running on the same route as shown earlier and is shown here at Tiryberth, with the garage in the background, and in revised livery.

1953

3	[9]	MTG 620	Leyland PD2/10	Leyland	L27/26R
12	[10]	MTG 883	AEC Regal III	Longwell Green	B35F
19	[11]	MTG 884	AEC Regal III	Longwell Green	B35F

Another double-decker was required in 1953 and again the order changed, resulting in the arrival of a Leyland Titan with lowbridge Leyland bodywork of traditional design: it lasted in service until 1971, showing the quality of the workmanship, and was then exported to the United States. It too was used mostly on the trunk service from Ystrad Mynach to Rhymney Bridge, running in excess of one million miles during its time in service. The two AECs had bodywork by Longwell Green, which was to become the Council's preferred supplier over the next few years, on Park Royal frames. They were rebuilt by the Council as late as 1966/7 but withdrawn in 1968-70. 11[19] passed initially to Henley of Abertillery, but was then sold for preservation, reappearing on the final day of Gelligaer operation. It was then placed on permanent loan to the National Museum of Wales, then the Welsh Industrial and Maritime Museum, and after the closure of that institution in 1998 it has apparently remained in store.

The first vehicles bodied for the Council by Longwell Green arrived in 1953. Number 12, later 10 (MTG 883), on AEC Regal III chassis, is seen at the garage at Tiryberth in 1967.

In 1954 the last two vertical-engined single-deckers arrived. Number 2, later 12, was one of the last AEC Regal III chassis supplied for the home market. The nearside of its Longwell Green bodywork is seen here in 1966.

1954

| 2 | [12] | OTG 320 | AEC Regal III | Longwell Green | B35F |
| 15 | [13] | OTG 321 | AEC Regal III | Longwell Green | B35F |

By October 1954, when these last Regals arrived, the purchase of new vertical engined single-deckers was becoming very unusual indeed. Apart from the special requirement of West Mon for the Bargoed Hill service, Gelligaer was the last municipal operator in the area to purchase such vehicles. The two lasted until 1967 without substantial rebuilding.

The offside of its fellow, No. 15, later 13 (OTG 321) is shown at Hanbury Square, Bargoed, to which it had worked from Ystrad Mynach via Cefn Hengoed in August 1956.

1955

| 27 | [14] | RTX 965 | AEC Reliance | Longwell Green | B44F |
| 28 | [15] | RTX 966 | AEC Reliance | Longwell Green | B44F |

In 1955 the Council finally took the plunge and bought its first underfloor-engined vehicles, which were also its first buses to be eight feet wide. Driver access was, unusually, through an offside door. They were never converted to one-man operation when the other, later, Reliances were modified. 28 was reseated to 42 from 1966 to 1968 during which time a luggage rack was fitted. They were both withdrawn and stripped for sale in 1970.

The unusual driver's offside door is well shown in this picture of AEC Reliance/Longwell Green No. 27, later 14 (RTX 965), one of Gelligaer's first underfloor-engined single-deckers, at Rhymney in 1956, when still new.

1957

16	-	VNY 254	AEC Reliance	Longwell Green	B44F
22	[17]	VNY 255	AEC Reliance	Longwell Green	B44F

A further two Reliances followed in 1957, both of which were converted to one-man operation. 16 was not renumbered because in the new sequence adopted by Roy Marshall in 1966, it was by chance the sixteenth vehicle in order of age. They were both withdrawn in 1972.

The next two Reliances to arrive had far more rounded bodies, also by Longwell Green. Number 16 (VNY 254) was not renumbered as it happened to fit into Roy Marshall's new scheme in its proper place. It was at Tiryberth in 1967.

1958

4	[18]	YTX 61	AEC Reliance	Longwell Green	B44F
5	[19]	YTX 62	AEC Reliance	Longwell Green	B44F

The successful combination of AEC chassis and Longwell Green bodywork was by this time established for single-deck deliveries: the small Bristol area builder was able to give proper service to a relatively small concern. 4 had a luggage rack fitted in 1966/7, reducing its capacity by 2 for that period. Both were equipped for one-man operation and survived to be the oldest Gelligaer vehicles transferred to Rhymney Valley in 1974.

In 1958 the Council took delivery of a further two Reliances with Longwell Green bodies. In 1964 No.4, later 18, (YTX 61) is at Bargoed, turning to pick up passengers for Ystrad Mynach via Gelligaer, with the massive slag heap which dominated the town in the background.

1959

7		[21]	359 CTX	Leyland PD2/40	Longwell Green	L27/28RD

The withdrawal of the first of the utility Daimlers in 1959 required the purchase of another double-decker: the Council stayed with Leyland for this despite its allegiance to AEC for single-deckers, but again specified bodywork by Longwell Green. This vehicle had power platform doors: although sections of the Ystrad Mynach-Bargoed-Rhymney Bridge service were urban, there were quite long sections of open and exposed moorland. In 1966 rebuilding was required because of a problem with the floor over the rear axle and this was carried out by Caerphilly UDC. The vehicle was withdrawn in November 1970 after suffering accident damage and was scrapped.

Another double-decker arrived in 1959, but by this time Leyland had long since given up constructing bodywork for its own chassis. Longwell Green built the body and for the first time platform doors were fitted. Number 7, later 21, (359 CTX) is at Tiryberth in 1966.

1960

14		[23]	751 HNY	Leyland PD2/40	Longwell Green	L27/28RD

The following year saw the withdrawal of the second of the Daimlers and the arrival of the second Leyland Titan with exposed radiator and platform doors. Unlike many of the double-deckers bodied for Newport, these vehicles did not feature a curved section above the driver's cab, which was a particular feature of Longwell Green bodies. This vehicle too was rebuilt by Caerphilly UDC in 1966/7. It was withdrawn in 1971.

1961

29	[24]		363 MTG	AEC Reliance	Longwell Green	B44F

This vehicle, as with 4, was reseated to 42 in 1966 but the luggage rack was removed the following year. It was the first AEC Reliance in the fleet which was adapted for one-man operation. It passed to Rhymney Valley in 1974.

1962

6	[25]	643 PTX	AEC Reliance	Longwell Green	B44F
30	[26]	644 PTX	AEC Reliance	Longwell Green	B44F

These vehicles were later converted to one-man operation and passed to RVDC. 30[26] was reseated like 29[24] and the rack was later removed.

In 1962 there was a reversion to purchasing two vehicles, which were similar to that which arrived the year before. Number 30, later 26, (644 PTX) is loading in Bargoed for the town service in 1964.

1963

10	[27]	889 UTG	AEC Reliance	Longwell Green	B44F
23	[28]	890 UTG	AEC Reliance	Longwell Green	B44F

The last two vehicles bodied by Longwell Green for the Council arrived in August 1963. Both were later converted to one-man operation and passed to RVDC.

In 1963 the last two vehicles constructed for the Council by Longwell Green were delivered. Number 23, later 28, (890 UTG) on the Pontypridd-Bedlinog service is followed by a West Mon vehicle on the Pontypridd-Blackwood route in 1966.

1964

24		[29]	ANY 432B	AEC Reliance	Willowbrook	B44F
13		[30]	ANY 433B	AEC Reliance	Willowbrook	B44F

The first two Willowbrook-bodied vehicles were also reseated and later had their luggage racks removed: they were also converted to one-man operation and then passed to RVDC.

The 1964 bodybuilding contract went to Willowbrook, who produced two vehicles not dissimilar to those made by Longwell Green. AEC Reliance No. 24, later 29, (ANY 432B) is seen outside the depot in 1967.

1965

9		[31]	ETX 388C	AEC Reliance	Willowbrook	B43F
18		[32]	ETX 389C	AEC Reliance	Willowbrook	B43F

These two vehicles were both reseated to B45F in 1967: they were later converted to one-man operation and passed to RVDC.

A further two Willowbrook-bodied Reliances arrived in 1965. In 1967, No. 9, later 31, (ETX 388C) was at Ystrad Mynach after arriving from Bargoed via Cefn Hengoed. It appears to have suffered some panel damage to the skirt.

1966

33	-	LTG 733D	AEC Reliance	Willowbrook	B42D
34	-	LTG 734D	AEC Reliance	Willowbrook	B42D
20	-	TJU 686	AEC Reliance	Duple Midland	B44F
22	-	UJU 774	AEC Reliance	Willowbrook	B45F

By 1966 the impetus to one-man operation was growing and 33 and 34 were delivered equipped with power-operated doors and full destination displays including provision for route numbers. They also reverted after very many years to dual entrance, but in 1971 were converted to B43F and in 1973 two extra seats were added. They were the last vehicles delivered in the red green and grey livery which had been used since the war. They passed to RVDC. 20 was new in 1959 and was originally a Duple demonstrator, passing to Jones Omnibus Services of Aberbeeg in 1960. The front was rebuilt after accident damage. It was withdrawn in 1972 after a further accident. 22 was new in 1960 and was originally a Willowbrook demonstrator, passing to Jones later that year. It lasted to be passed to RVDC. The Council acquired a third former Jones Reliance with Duple Midland body, NCJ 108, which was used for spares only.

In 1966 two further new Reliances arrived, also with Willowbrook bodies, but they had full destination displays and were originally provided with dual-entrances, as seen here. In 1969 No. 34 (LTG 734D) was caught at Glyngaer on the short double run off the main road: it was running through to Heolddu Drive.

Duple Midland-bodied AEC Reliance No. 20 was rebuilt with a more angular front, following accident damage. In July 1969 it was pictured at Cefn Hengoed on service 5.

The second Reliance acquired from Jones was No. 22 (UJU 774) which was also a demonstrator, in its case for Willowbrook. It was one of the first vehicles converted for one-man operation and is seen at Tiryberth in 1968.

1967

35		-	FGW 498C	AEC Swift	Willowbrook	B53F
36		-	STB 957C	Leyland PSUR1/1R	Willowbrook	B53F

The new order arrived in 1967, with the purchase of two rear-engined single-deckers, both former demonstrators. The AEC Swift was on loan twice during 1966, and was then purchased very cheaply from the manufacturers. It was fitted for one-man operation before entering service in May 1967. It introduced to the fleet both air operated doors and fluorescent lighting. In 1969 it was painted in a special livery to commemorate the investiture of HRH Prince Charles at Caernarvon. It was transferred to RVDC. The other vehicle new that year was a Leyland Panther: a shorter Panther Cub had been demonstrated in 1966, but the longer version was acquired in May 1967 and shortly thereafter adapted for omo. The Panther was a generally unsuccessful design and this one was sold as early as 1972, ostensibly for further service in Afghanistan. However, it in fact ran in this country for a few more years.

1968

51	-	PTX 451F	Austin LM30	Gelligaer	M12
37	-	TTX 37G	AEC Swift	Willowbrook	B49D
38	-	TTX 38G	AEC Swift	Willowbrook	B49D

The arrivals in 1968 contrasted. In February the Council acquired an Austin van and fitted it with windows and perimeter seating: it replaced a Morris LD05 minibus which had been acquired in 1961 and was scrapped in 1967 after being involved in an accident. However, while the Morris had not been licensed as a PSV, the Austin was. At the end of the year, two further Swifts arrived, the first vehicles to be delivered in the new livery introduced that year: dark green roof, red lower parts and white around the windows. Both were rebuilt to B54F in 1972 and survived to pass to RVDC.

Another former demonstrator was AEC Swift No. 35 (FGW 498C) with Willowbrook B53F body. In 1969 it was painted in a special livery for Prince Charles' investiture and is shown thus at Glyngaer, wrongly displaying the route number 5 instead of 2 for the Ystrad Mynach-Bargoed via Gelligaer service.

The second acquisition in 1967 was Leyland Panther No. 36 (STB 957C), which was to stay only for five years. Here it is seen amid snowy conditions climbing up from Pontlottyn to Fochriw on service 8.

An unusual arrival in 1968 was an Austin minibus No. 51 (PTX 451F) with a body fitted in the Council's own workshop: it replaced a Morris which had not been licenced for use as a PSV. It is shown when brand new, outside the garage.

Also in 1968 the Council bought two new Swifts, which were the first vehicles in the fleet to be delivered in the new livery with a green roof and white lower areas. The year after arriving No. 38 (TTX 38G) was at Glyngaer on service 2 to Bargoed.

1971

39		BTX 539J	Bristol VRTSL6G	Northern Counties	H44/33F
40		BTX 540J	Bristol VRTSL6G	Northern Counties	H44/33F
41		BTX 541J	Bristol VRTSL6G	Northern Counties	H44/33F
21		YNY 922	Leyland PD2/40	Massey	L29/28R

The introduction of the larger vehicles meant that the fleet did not require any new stock for 1969 or 1970, although the severe winter of 1970/1 meant that a number of vehicles had to be hired in to cover for those damaged. However, in 1971 four double-deckers arrived. The three Bristols were needed because of the increased demands caused by the through running to Newport, and were far larger in capacity than any vehicles owned before. They were crew operated. Gelligaer jumped ahead of the other small South Wales municipalities by taking delivery of rear-engined double-deckers. The Leyland Titan was new to Caerphilly UDC in 1958 and was acquired after being loaned: it was painted into Gelligaer livery by Western Welsh. It replaced the first of the two Longwell Green-bodied Titans, which had to be withdrawn after accident damage, but it lasted only until 1972 with Gelligaer.

One of the three Northern Counties-bodied Bristol VRs of 1971 No. 41 (BTX 541J) was caught in Caerphilly the following year heading for Newport: new territory for Gelligaer.

1972

42	-	KTX 242L	Bristol RESL6G	ECW	B47F
43	-	KTX 243L	Bristol RESL6G	ECW	B47F
44	-	KTX 244L	Bristol RESL6G	ECW	B47F
23	-	OTG 518	Leyland PSU1/13	Massey	B44F
20	-	LKG 664	AEC Regent V	Park Royal	L31/28RD
100	-	WKG 281	AEC Reliance	Willowbrook	DP41F
101	-	WKG 284	AEC Reliance	Willowbrook	DP41F

1972 saw the arrival of no fewer than seven vehicles, three new and four second hand. The three new vehicles were the first batch of Bristol REs pre-ordered during Roy Marshall's tenure of the managership, and they passed to RVDC in 1974. 23 was new to Caerphilly UDC in 1954: before it arrived, similar vehicle

9 was also bought and was cannibalised to revitalise it. It was purchased as a short term replacement for 20, which was withdrawn after an accident and was itself withdrawn before the end of the year. The Regent V was new to Western Welsh in 1956 and was largely used for training drivers in the use of manual gearboxes. It was sold shortly before the formation of the RVDC. The remaining two Reliances were also new to Western Welsh, but in 1961, and were purchased for private hire use. Both were painted in pale green, white and red and were passed to RVDC.

Bristol RE with Eastern Coach Works body No. 42 is seen in Rhymney on the long run to Newport, about to pick up a girl in what can now be regarded as period costume.

In 1972 No. 23 (OTG 518), an 18-year-old Leyland with Massey body, was bought from neighbours Caerphilly as a short term measure. It is seen that year at Fiddler's Elbow on the Bedlinog-Pontypridd service inherited from Jones of Treharris.

On the same day, No. 23 was seen at the small bus station at Nelson.

Also in 1972 the Council acquired a 1956 AEC Regent from Western Welsh, which was largely used thereafter for driver training, although it was properly painted. Number 20 (LKG 664) is outside the depot.

The final acquisitions in 1972 were two 1961 Reliances with Willowbrook dual-purpose bodies, which also came from Western Welsh. They were bought for private hire, but here No. 101 (WKG 284) is seen in 1973 at Hanbury Square on the Blackwood service run jointly with West Mon.

The other Reliance acquired from Western Welsh was No. 100 (WKG 100), which appears to have had its front modified. It is shown on stage service in Bargoed in late 1973.

102		-	DKG 887L	Bedford YRQ	Duple	C45F
45		-	NKG 245M	Bristol RESL6G	ECW	DP44F
46		-	NKG 246M	Bristol RESL6G	ECW	DP44F
47		-	NKG 247M	Bristol RESL6G	ECW	DP44F
103		-	RTG 221M	Bedford YRT	Duple	C53F

1973 saw the arrival of five vehicles. The Bedford YRQ was delivered in April 1973 in all-over cream livery and was intended for private hire: however, as early as December 1973 it was withdrawn and replaced by the YRT, which was purchased with a bus grant and used partly on service. The latter had a white livery with pale blue flash. In October 1973 the second batch of Bristol REs arrived, with dual-purpose bodies featuring high-back seats. 45 was very soon involved in a serious accident and was rebuilt by Red & White in early 1974. These three were painted white, with green skirt and a red band below the windows. They and the second Bristol all passed to RVDC.

One of the shortest lived of the Council's vehicles was No. 102 (DKG 887L), a Bedford YRQ with Duple C45F body which was designed for private hire work and was delivered in April 1973 in an all over cream livery. It is seen here at Tiryberth in September of that year, but had gone by December.

In December 1973 the Bedford YRQ was replaced by No. 103 (RTG 221M), a Bedford YRT with Duple C53F body, which was purchased with a bus grant. It was thus used sometimes on stage service, as here in November 1974 at Rhymney Bridge.

Number 47 (NKG 247M) was loaned to Burton, Roy Marshall's new undertaking, and was seen there in February 1974.

1974

10	-	RAX 583	AEC Regent V	Massey	L29/28R

The last vehicle acquired by Gelligaer was new to Bedwas & Machen in 1957 and although fleetnames were applied, it retained its B & M livery. It passed to RVDC. Similar vehicle UWO 498 was on loan in January 1974.

The last vehicle purchased by the Council was AEC Regent V/Massey RAX 583, which was acquired from Bedwas & Machen and retained its former fleet number of 10. It acquired Gelligaer fleet names but retained its Bedwas livery: it is seen here in August 1974 bearing its Rhymney Valley number, 83.

TICKET SELECTION

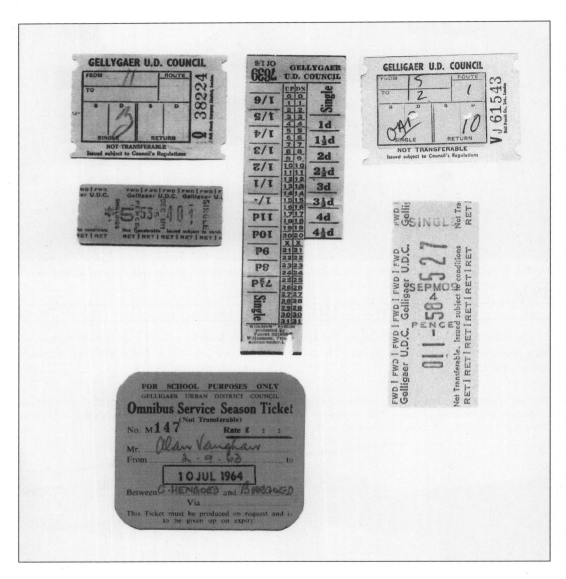

DESCRIPTION

Top left: Bellgraphic. Fare written in by conductor.

Top centre: Willebrew. Denotes fare paid on side of cut away portion of ticket

Top right: As top left but note change of spelling for Gelligaer

Centre left: Setright Speed

Foot: School Pass. Probably renewable every term

Lower right: Setright Speed, different colour and enlarged for clarity